TRUE BEARING

A Memoir

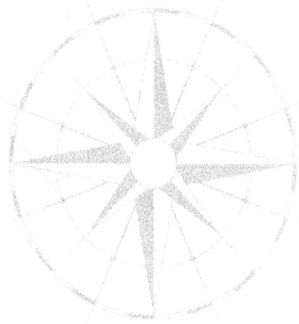

TRUE BEARING

A Memoir

Terrie Dorfman

LIP PUBS TRADE PAPERBACKS

CROCKETT, CALIFORNIA

ISBN: 978-0-9846339-2-0
Library of Congress Control Number: 2011946251
Designed by Carol Sevilla
Printed in the United States of America

*To my sons, Brock and Kent, for your support through the
years. I am proud of you both.*

ACKNOWLEDGMENTS

*I truly want to thank my good friend and author, Jeri Ferris.
Her enthusiasm about my story encouraged me to write*
True Bearing.

*My special thanks go to Sue Clark, my editor, advisor, critic
and now my special friend. Her patience, interest, understanding
and never ending wisdom made writing my story
a much easier task.*

*I am grateful for the support and encouragement of my
husband, Herb, and my family.*

True bearing: An absolute bearing using true north.

Introduction

A gentle wind floated across sunny San Francisco Bay, a perfect day for sailing. Herb and I were enjoying every minute of that summer afternoon in 1979 as our 30' sloop Golconda glided in silence through the calm waters.

We were admiring the dozens of beautiful boats on the Bay when I spotted a three hulled trimaran.

"Herb, please try to steer closer so I can read the name on the transom of that trimaran over there," I said.

"I'll try to get over, but I doubt it's your trimaran, if that's what you're thinking."

When I read Cold Duck, the name her new owners had christened her, I knew she was the trimaran Frank and I had built. I'd know her anywhere.

She was sailing toward the Golden Gate Bridge. She looked so seaworthy, a graceful sight as she continued out to sea. As I watched her, my heart filled with memories.

My name is Terrie. This is my story.

TRUE BEARING

A Memoir

Chapter 1

Life began for me, Frances Teresa Allen, on October 27, 1924 when my mom gave birth to twin daughters in the bedroom of our family home in Nottingham, England. The babies were so tiny that Dr. Taylor gave Bertha and Frank Allen little hope for the twins' survival.

My little sister died a few hours after birth, but I'm told I was determined not to give up. I surprised everyone by living through the night.

A few days later, Dr. Taylor said, "Well, Bertha, you and Frank have a stubborn little daughter. Although she's not very strong, it looks like she's going to live."

I gained weight and strength, growing into a wee dark-haired baby with bright brown eyes and a happy disposition, or so my mom told me.

My parents had two other children, ten-year-old Billy and two-year-old Kathleen. My brother was dark-haired, too, round-faced with deep green eyes, and energetic with a quick temper. Kathleen, a pretty light-brown-haired child, had a typical English complexion with rosy cheeks and blue eyes. Although Kathleen loved me, her baby sister, I was told she showed some resentment at the attention others gave me because I was delicate and needed extra care.

Soon, it became apparent that my mother needed help with the children and the housework. Daddy suggested hiring a nursemaid. After interviewing a number of applicants, Mom hired Edith Wallwork, an elderly spinster with a warm smile. She wore her white hair piled on top of her head in a neat bun. Edith's light blue eyes seemed to sparkle when she smiled. Her references were excellent.

Soon Edith was settled into her own room in our family home and before long, Mom and Dad knew they'd made the right choice. She was a hard worker with a world of patience. Billy and Kathleen liked her at once, I'm told.

My mom wouldn't allow Edith to hold me. She was very possessive of the baby she'd almost lost. However, one day, as she was preparing to go to her bridge club, Mom called Edith into the living room. "I have to leave you with the children for a few hours, Edith."

"Yes, Ma'am."

"Since Billy's in school and Kathleen's napping, do you think you can manage little Frances Teresa?"

Edith was delighted. "Oh, Mrs. Allen. I'll be happy to take care of the children while you're out. Please go and have a nice afternoon. Don't worry. Everything will be just fine here."

When Edith lifted me out of my crib I snuggled, contented,

in her arms. I knew Edith's heart filled with love at that moment, because that's just who Edith was.

The years passed and Edith and I grew closer. We spent hours together in front of the big fireplace in the kitchen while Edith read to me and told me her wonderful stories.

Through the years, our family stories always included the one about how Mom sensed I was depending on Edith more than on her and she was concerned. However, Kathleen was happy to get more attention from her mother, and Billy was busy with his friends and didn't depend on Edith or our parents for company. So, peace reigned in the family when Edith was with us.

I continued to be a delicate child. I tired easily and seemed to have little resistance to childhood ills. When I was six, Dr. Taylor suggested dancing lessons might give me more stamina. Mom looked into various schools and selected Miss Palmer's School for Beginning Ballet.

Miss Palmer had studied with the world famous ballerina, Anna Pavlova, famous for her performance as the dying swan in "Swan Lake." Miss Palmer was very strict and demanded perfection in posture and balance.

I soon advanced enough to dance "on toe." Miss Palmer delighted in the recitals her students presented each year. Mom made beautiful costumes for me, including tutus and long ballet skirts, all in lovely colors. I never ceased being thrilled with the lights, music and applause. I admit I loved the flowers and gifts I received from my family and friends after my performances. I made up my mind that one day I'd be a famous dancer and perform for audiences all over the world.

Edith took me to my lesson each week. I loved the class.

I quickly learned the steps and would practice them at home. Before long, I begged my parents to allow me to attend two classes a week. Miss Palmer, happy and enthusiastic with my progress, told my parents I showed an aptitude for ballet.

By the time I was eight, I decided to change my name from Frances Teresa to Terrie. I thought Frances Teresa was too formal and too saintly. Besides, Frances Teresa didn't seem to fit a small, delicate little girl like me. Mom didn't like my decision, but at least she agreed to call me by my middle name.

I adored my brother. I'd run errands for Billy, and he and his friends would allow me to watch them play ball or practice their boxing in the garage. I can remember wishing I'd been born a boy, but then I'd remember my dancing and be glad to be a girl.

Kathleen and I were good friends even though we had very different dispositions and ideas. Kathleen was more ladylike than I. She was tall, very pretty, enjoyed school and didn't have my vivid imagination.

Nottingham, in the Midlands north of London, has a beautiful downtown shopping area with an elegant town hall. Lace factories have always been the city's main industry.

Many small subdivisions make up the residential part of Nottingham, including Sherwood where my family lived. We had a lovely house with five bedrooms upstairs and a large bathroom with a separate lavatory. Downstairs, we had a sitting room, dining room, office, kitchen, scullery and pantry, plus an impressive entry hall.

The master bedroom was the largest of the five upstairs rooms. Kathleen and I shared a bedroom, Bill and Edith each had their own rooms and the other was a spare bedroom. I used the spare bedroom to practice dancing when the room was not in use.

The kitchen had a big fireplace heated by coal. Above it was a clothes rack that we could pull up over the fireplace to dry our clothes. The kitchen had a separate door that opened into the coal cellar. We had a dining table in the kitchen, but my parents always ate in the formal dining room. Edith ate in the kitchen. If we had guests, Kathleen and I ate with Edith.

The family used the scullery to cook in as well as for washing the dishes and doing the laundry. The pantry, off the kitchen, had shelves for food, plus marble shelves for keeping things cold.

The house was built of brick and had beautiful bay windows. The front entrance had steps leading up to the door. A path led from the back door to the garage. A wood fence on three sides of the yard enclosed a rock garden that sat in the center of the backyard with a fish pond in the middle, as well as two apple trees, rose bushes, shrubs and flower beds. Mother had a greenhouse at the bottom of the garden where she grew flowers for the house.

When I was nine, Miss Palmer recommended that my parents enroll me in a special ballet school. I'd be instructed by a representative from the Royal School of Ballet. If the school accepted me, I'd train for examinations that took place twice a year in London. If a student was exceptionally talented, she'd eventually be given the opportunity to audition for a place in the famous Royal Ballet Company.

I was ecstatic, but my parents were hesitant to let me devote more time to dancing because I was neglecting my school work. I was determined to go on with my dancing.

Actually, I was a good student, I just didn't enjoy school. When I was 12, I accepted the chance to take the required exam to go to a higher academic level. If I passed the exam, I would be eligible to continue school at that higher level when I was 14. Much to my parent's and my amazement, I passed the test.

I continued in the public school until June. I was still only twelve. In September, 1936, my parents enrolled me in the Sacred Heart Convent for one year. We were not a Catholic family, but Mom heard that the nuns were excellent and strict teachers. Those nuns didn't take kindly to my excuses for late homework assignments. I did make an effort to do better, but my dancing lessons and practices made me neglect my school work.

Students had the legal right to leave school at 14. I was to be 14 in October, 1938, and I decided not to return to school in September, even though I had passed the exam, I decided to get a job instead.

My parents were not happy with my decision. "You'll be sorry one day," Dad said. "A good education is very important, but we can't make you study, so maybe a job will be good for you."

I worked in the stockroom of a department store for a year and managed to get to London twice that year. I completed five exams for ballet with high marks. I hoped one day I might earn a place in the Royal Ballet.

But that was not to be. In 1939, England declared war with Germany and I was no longer allowed to travel to London.

I've always loved animals. For a while, I worked at the People's Dispensary for Sick Animals (PDSA), where they said they'd train me if I wanted to be a vet. I loved the job, but in

1939, people were having their pets put down because they were afraid they would not be able to feed their animals in war years. I stayed for a while until I couldn't handle seeing healthy animals destroyed.

During those years, I loved to read about faraway places and dreamed of traveling to cities all over the world. Edith listened to my dreams and would tell me, "Follow your dreams, darling, and when you really believe you are right, never give up."

Chapter 2

When the war reached England, my parents remembered what World War I had been like and they feared what another conflict with Germany would mean. They knew this war would be much worse. England was totally unprepared.

Prime Minister Neville Chamberlain had returned from Europe two years earlier, assuring the British people that Germany wanted peace, but the promise had already proven false. Poland had been invaded and Europe was in turmoil. The British knew Chamberlain was wrong.

England's new Prime Minister, Winston Churchill, declared England at war with Germany in 1939. We were determined not to allow our little island to be invaded. We began preparations for a fight.

The Royal Air Force fliers were in the sky day and night. The Halifax and Spitfire fighter planes overcame the first German attacks. The Battle of Britain had begun.

The Blitz was yet to come. Industrial cities were the main targets. Nottingham was not severely damaged, but due to the many airfields nearby, we saw a lot of action. Planes left on missions around the clock.

I knew in my heart that the Germans would never set foot on English soil. Mom told Kathleen and me that she would never let the Germans capture us. She said she'd give us a "pill" first. When she said that, I began to understand the seriousness of war.

The Germans overtook France in 1940 when Dunkirk was invaded and the evacuation of British troops from France was necessary. The troops waited on those French beaches to be picked up by all manner of ships — warships, private and fishing boats, anything that could get them back to England.

When the rescued soldiers arrived in England, they needed places to stay. A billeting officer came to our house to see how many of the men who had just arrived from Dunkirk could stay in our home until they could be taken to their barracks. Mom said we could take two of the soldiers. She sent me with the officer to bring the men to our house. They were so young and appeared to be almost in shock as they sat in front of the fire in our kitchen. They refused to go into our living room because they felt they were beneath our family's social class. My heart was sad when I realized they felt that way. Those boys were willing to die for my family and for our country.

I'll never forget seeing that line of young soldiers. They were so tired, dirty, beaten and sad. I knew then how terrible war was. I wondered why countries couldn't live at peace with each other.

Our life and values changed drastically. Families were split up—sons and daughters went to war, children were moved out

of populated cities like London to safer areas in the country, and
vegetable gardens replaced our flower beds. Civilians who were
not eligible for the military became air raid wardens.

When the war came to Britain, the first order was for
everyone to get blackout material to cover every window and
areas where light could be seen at night. We were given gas
masks and the government issued clothing coupons and food
stamps.

Everyone quickly learned that we'd have to be more efficient
in making meals without meat. Dad had an allotment — a piece
of ground where he could grow potatoes, carrots, turnips, cabbage
and beets. He also raised a couple of chickens, but he was
required to give some of the eggs to the government.

We ate a lot of rabbit, fresh fruit and vegetables, colored lard
and puddings made with powdered milk. Even so, eating was not
the most important part of everyone's day.

I remember when a Polish family moved into the house next
door. They had escaped from their country when Hitler overtook
Poland. The mother and father spoke little English. They were
well-educated and extremely grateful to be alive. They had two
sons –- Jochiam, age 15 and Michel, 11.

Jochiam and I became good friends. When the sirens
sounded, we'd climb onto the house roof with kitchen pots on our
heads in case flak fell on us. We liked to watch the searchlights
play across the night sky. We talked for hours about our lives in
our different parts of the world. And we always wondered when
the war would end.

In 1937, Billy, 23, married Marjorie Edwards, a charming,
slender blond girl. I adored her. In 1939, Billy tried to enlist in
the Royal Air Force. He wasn't accepted due to a vision problem.

So, he joined the Army. They assigned him to a medical unit and
sent him to North Africa to fight under Field Marshall Bernard
Montgomery in the desert campaign against German Field
Marshall Erwin Rommel, better known as the Desert Fox.

Billy was carrying a wounded man on a stretcher when he
stepped on a loaded rifle. A bullet went into his ankle. He was
sent home in 1941. General "Monty" Montgomery defeated the
Desert Fox on November 4, 1943.

After Billy and Marjorie were married, they bought a sweet
and ice cream shop in Nottingham. When Billy went away to war,
Marjorie couldn't get supplies for the store and after a while, it
became too much for her to handle alone. She sold the shop, and
went to live with her parents. I tried to see her as often as I could
to keep her company. We both missed Billy. He was given an
honorable discharge in 1940.

Mom spent hours knitting for servicemen. She organized
drives to raise money for war widows and helped with other
worthy causes. Our house was open to any serviceman who
needed a place to stay when he was on leave.

Kathleen was now seventeen and old enough to enlist in the
Women's Air Force (WAF). She trained to become a plotter and
was stationed at a base near Nottingham. Her duties were to use
a pointer on a huge map to show the locations of German and
British aircraft.

I soon became frustrated. I'd discontinued my ballet lessons
because my parents wouldn't let me go out during the blackouts
at the time when all of my classes were scheduled. I wanted some
excitement and thought it would be great to enlist in the service
and become an ambulance driver. I was turned away at various
recruiting offices because I was just 15.

Edith had decided to leave our family as she had become too old to help with the housework, and besides, the children were all grown.

Mom and Dad insisted Edith was still part of the family and that she'd always have a home with us. However, our old nurse was independent and refused to stay. She moved into a tiny apartment a few miles from our home. I stopped in often for tea and I'd tell Edith how unhappy I was. She listened patiently and would tell me, "You must keep practicing your dancing. It'll be useful to you one day. The war cannot last forever, so don't be in such a hurry to grow up."

As I left Edith's apartment in Nottingham one afternoon, I noticed the YMCA across the street from Victoria Station. I hurried to the building, found the office and asked to see the manager. A lady showed me to another room and introduced me to a tall, dark-haired young man, who introduced himself as Jim Edgar. "What can I do for you," he asked.

"Well," I said, "I'm trying to find something worthwhile to do to help the war effort. Would you have any opening in the service canteen?"

"We do have some jobs available, but you have to be eighteen to work here."

I crossed my fingers behind my back and said, "That's no problem."

"You look younger than eighteen, Terrie,"

I didn't say anything.

"As a matter of fact, Mamie, our canteen manager, does need an assistant. She has a crew of women who work as volunteers a few hours a week. If you're willing to work hard, I'm sure we could use you. Let me call her."

Mamie Anderson was a plain girl with a warm smile, about 28 and very pleasant. When Jim told her his plan for hiring me, she was delighted. "It'll be great to have you. Things get really hectic around here at times."

"The salary at the YMCA is minimal, Terrie," Jim said. "This is not a rich organization."

I told him I still lived at home with my parents, so that wasn't a problem. I decided to worry about that later.

Jim showed me the kitchen and dining area, and the recreation room used by the young Y members. The rec room was equipped with billiards, table tennis, cards and chess. The Y also had a well-stocked library and a piano. The bedrooms and bathrooms were on the second floor and were available to servicemen for a nominal fee.

Jim introduced me to the office staff. I met Miss Richeson, a middle-aged spinster with reddish hair and twinkling blue eyes. Everyone called her Richie. The other secretary, Madge Kennedy, was a short, plump girl with dark hair. I later learned that Madge's husband, George, was an RAF flyer stationed overseas. The Y had a large reception hall on the ground floor that they used for occasional meetings or dances.

I could hardly wait to start my job. At the same time, I was apprehensive when I told my parents what I'd done. They were not happy.

"You were wrong to tell Mr. Edgar that you were eighteen," Dad told me. "He'll not like it when he finds out you lied. However, we know you've made up your mind so go ahead and try." Mom and Dad knew that once I decided to do something, I wouldn't give up.

My job at the Y was to arrange menus, order supplies, register servicemen for rooms and help in the kitchen when the work was too heavy for volunteer helpers. I put in many extra hours and often had to walk the three miles home when I missed the last bus.

During the war, there were no buses after dark, but I wasn't afraid to walk home during a blackout. When the air raid sirens wailed, I'd stand in a doorway and watch the searchlights. I could hear the gunfire in the distance and the flak when it fell near me on the street. This real life adventure had become a way of life in Britain. To me, life had always been like this.

Sometimes a serviceman would walk home with me to stay in our spare room if there were no rooms at the Y. No matter when I got home, the door was always unlocked. People trusted each other during those war years.

One night, as I worked at the reception desk, I heard a voice say, "Hello, Miss. Is there a chance of a room for a weary Canadian?"

I looked up to see a tall, heavyset man wearing the uniform of the RCAF. He had a round face with a pleasant smile.

"Oh, I'm sorry. All the rooms are taken for tonight." I saw the disappointment on his face, so I added, "But my parents would be happy to have you stay at our house if that's all right with you. If you're in a hurry, you can catch the last bus. I'll call to tell them you're coming."

"That sounds great, but I'll wait until you're ready to leave and then you can show me the way. Okay?"

"I'll be here for another hour, and then I'll be walking home. The buses don't run after seven."

"Would it be all right if I wait for you?"

I felt the sincerity in the airman's voice. "If you'd like. I'd be happy to have company. Why don't you wait in the boys club until I'm ready to leave?"

As we walked to my house, I learned the airman's name was Frank Dagg. He came from Winnipeg, a large city in the prairie province of Manitoba. He was the youngest of eleven brothers and sisters who had raised him after his parents died when he was three. Frank told me he was a mid-upper turret gunner on a British Lancaster bomber and was stationed at an airbase not too far from Nottingham.

"I've always wanted to fly," he said. "I came to England in 1936 to try to join the RAF, but they wouldn't accept me because I didn't have the necessary education. I went back to Canada and two years later joined the RCAF."

Frank had wanted to be a pilot, but he failed the navigator's exam by three points, so they sent him to England as a gunner. Many of the men who came over with his unit had already been killed or were missing.

"As soon as I complete my second tour of operations, I plan to try for my wings again. I have two ambitions," he told me. "One is to be a commercial airline pilot and the other is to build my own boat and sail around the world."

"Really?"

"Yes, ma'am. I know this all sounds unrealistic, but if we don't have goals and dreams, we're fighting this war for nothing."

I was impressed by this interesting airman. "I have a dream, too," I said. "I intend to continue my dancing career with a ballet company and travel around the world. There's so much I want to see."

By the time we reached the house, I felt as if I'd known Frank much longer than a few hours. When I introduced Frank to Mom and Dad, I was pleased with the warmth of their greeting. They'd allowed many servicemen to use the house, but Frank Dagg seemed to be special.

Chapter 3

Since Frank soon became a regular visitor to the Allen household, he'd bring treats to share with the family from the care packages his sisters and brothers in Canada sent him. The sweets and biscuits were a rare treat in wartime England.

Frank was a heavy smoker and when his family sent cigarettes, he'd always bring a pack for Mom since she enjoyed a good cigarette, another difficult product to find in wartime England.

I saw a lot of Frank. I'd had many infatuations, but the way I felt about Frank seemed different. I found myself thinking of him all the time. When Frank didn't come into the Y, or I didn't hear from him for a few days, I worried and waited for the phone to ring. I didn't tell my parents how I felt, but one day I did confide in Edith.

"It sounds as if you're falling in love, dear," counseled my wise old friend.

I knew I mustn't let my feelings for Frank affect me. I had to keep busy with other things to keep my mind off Frank. I'd seen too many of my girlfriends get hurt over a wartime romance. The young soldiers were either lonely or just looking for temporary affairs until they could return to their wives back home. Some of my girlfriend's affairs ended when their lovers were killed or were listed as missing in action.

As the weeks went by, Frank and I found time to visit many of the historic places in Nottingham, including Newstead Abbey, the home of poet Lord Byron. The beautiful grounds feature a lake covered with water lilies. White swans swam gracefully on the water.

We also toured Nottingham Castle, in the center of the city, the setting for the famous Robin Hood legend.

The oldest inn in England, in later years called The Trip to Jerusalem, had been built into the rocks under Nottingham Castle. Crusaders met at the inn in the 1300s before they left for the Holy Land.

Frank was fascinated with Nottingham, the castle, the old inn and the story of Robin Hood.

Before long, I realized my love for Frank was growing. I could tell he felt the same way. One day, after a picnic on the grounds of Newstead Abbey, Frank took my hand and said, "Honey, we have to stop seeing so much of each other. We must not allow ourselves to become more than good friends. I'm eight years older than you and I come from a country three thousand miles away."

Oh, no. Was this really happening? My heart pounded as I knew what Frank was going to say.

"I'll be taking part in a lot of raids over Germany, Terrie.

We're caught up in a wartime romance. We can't allow our feelings to get out of hand. You'll just get hurt and I don't want that to happen."

I took a deep breath. "Can we still see each other once in a while? I'll try to be away from the house when you visit Mom and Dad, but please do see them. They're so fond of you."

I worked a lot of extra hours so I wouldn't meet Frank by accident. I tried hard to hide my love for him even from myself.

One evening, when I arrived home after a busy day at work, I found Frank in the living room having tea with my mother.

"Come in, dear," Mom said. "Frank has been telling me he'll not be seeing us for a while."

"I'm not permitted to give you any information," Frank said, "but I'll get in touch with you just as soon as I can. Don't be concerned if you don't hear from me for a few weeks."

I felt my heart beat faster as I strained to keep from showing my anxiety. I tried to be lighthearted as I said, "I have something for you. I've been wanting to give it to you for quite some time, but we haven't seen much of you, lately." I handed Frank a small, fluffy brown teddy bear. "This is for good luck."

"Well, thank you. He looks like a real friend. I'll call him Teddie and I'll carry him with me on all the raids."

The next few nights were long as we realized something important was happening in England. I was right. One evening, as I left the Y, I heard the roar of airplane engines and looked up to see the sky black with planes. It was June 1, 1942, and 1000 bombers were headed across the sea on a bombing raid. Some people actually thought England was being abandoned.

The armada flew east to Cologne where they dropped 3000 tons of bombs. The Germans called it "Flaming June." In ninety minutes, the powerful industrial area of Cologne had been destroyed, including military installations and factories.

The next news broadcast I heard from London told us that every available aircraft had taken part in that raid. Later, we learned of the unbelievable number of airmen who had been lost that night.

I knew Frank had been part of that raid. I feared he might not come back.

I was busy at the Y's reception desk a few nights later when I heard his voice.

"Hi, honey. Did you miss me?"

I ran into Frank's waiting arms. "Thank God you're safe," I said. "I was so worried. I knew you had gone on the Cologne raid. It must have been terrible."

"Terrie, I swear I'll never forget that night. We must have killed many innocent women and children while we were destroying the military targets. This war is so senseless."

Frank's eyes never left my face.

"By the way, I tied my good luck teddy bear to my guns and he didn't let me down."

I had tears in my eyes, picturing that night in Frank's plane.

"Honey," he said. "I now know I was wrong. I love you and if you feel the same way, we shouldn't hide our feelings."

A smile returned to my face. I hugged him tighter.

"We can't be married until this damn war is over, but I want to plan for our future together, anyway."

I laughed and cried at the same time. "We can wait, Frank. We have all the time in the world," I said.

My heart was light as we said goodbye when Frank had to return to his base. A few weeks later, I answered the phone at work to hear Frank's voice.

"Can you meet me at Victoria Station? I just have an hour between trains, but I have important news for you."

I met Frank at the ticket window. We found a bench and sat close to each other. "Please don't keep me in suspense," I said. "What's the news?"

"Well, it seems I've been awarded the Distinguished Flying Medal for my part in the Cologne raid. King George, himself, will present it to me at Buckingham Palace. I'm allowed two guests at the Investiture. I want you to come. I'm also inviting an old friend of mine, Gwen Howard. She manages a hostel in London."

"I'm so proud of you," I said. My heart burst with pride. "I'd be honored to be there. When will it be?"

Frank didn't have a date, yet, but he said it would be in the early afternoon. "You'll have to meet me in London. I'll be staying at Gwen's hostel. We'll arrange for a hotel room for you. The next morning, I'll put you back on a train for Nottingham."

I couldn't wait to tell Mom and Dad. I knew how proud they would be.

"I wish I could tell them in person, but I've been assigned to another base for special training, so I won't be in Nottingham again until after the Investiture. I'll be writing to ask their permission to marry you when the war's over."

We hugged. I didn't want to let go.

"In the meantime," Frank said, "I'll keep in touch and let you know the exact date and all the other details as soon as I have them. Remember, I love you. One day we'll be together for always, and we can start building our sailboat."

I could hardly wait to get home so I could tell my parents the news. Their reaction was one I never expected.

"Are you telling us that you intend to meet Frank in London and stay there overnight?" my dad said.

"Daddy, you make it sound very different than it is. In order to be there in time for the Investiture, I'll have to catch the early train. There isn't a train leaving London for Nottingham in the evening, so I'll take the first train home the next morning. Frank has a friend who manages a hostel in London, so he'll be staying there, and I'll get a hotel room."

My voice filled with excitement. "Frank asked me to marry him when the war's over. He'll be writing to ask your permission. He's taking special training in Wales or he'd be here himself."

Mother turned to me. "Well, young lady, you do not have our permission to go to London or to be married. You are not old enough to make these decisions for yourself."

Then, my dad added his opinion to Mom's. "Your mother is right, Terrie. You're just a child. Frank is too old for you, and he's from a country on the other side of the world. I'm disappointed in him for putting these ideas in your head. He's no longer welcome in this house and I forbid you to have anything more to do with him."

I stared at Dad. "Daddy, we love each other. I'm eighteen and not a child. We're willing to wait until after the war." I was talking to two angry parents. "You're not being fair. Frank and I tried hard not to see each other because we know how shallow wartime romances can be. Please try to understand and give us your blessing. I thought you would be so proud when Frank was awarded the Distinguished Flying Medal."

"We have told you our feelings, Teresa," Mom said. "We won't change our minds. If you go to London, you'll be disobeying us. We'll never consent to your marriage to Frank, Teresa. As far as we're concerned, the matter is closed."

I cried myself to sleep that night. When I arrived for work the following morning, Mamie questioned me.

"Terrie, is something wrong? You look as if you didn't sleep all night. Has something happened to Frank?"

My voice broke as I told Mamie about my confrontation with my parents.

"Well, dear, congratulations are in order. The opportunity to go to Buckingham Palace only happens once in a lifetime. You must go."

I hugged Mamie, so thankful to know someone agreed with me.

"You and Frank seem so right for each other. It's too bad you have to wait to get married."

I thanked Mamie for her encouragement. I made it through the day feeling much better. After work, I hurried to see Edith. Over a cup of tea, I told her the events of the past two days.

Edith listened. Finally, she took me in her arms and said, "Well, dear, you know I would never encourage you to go against the wishes of your parents, but you deserve this chance to go to London and see Frank decorated by King George. It's something you'll always remember. I'm surprised by the way your parents are behaving. They should know you well enough to realize that you won't do anything wrong if you stay overnight in London."

I hung on to Edith's every word. She was who I needed and I hugged her.

"Frank's a fine young man and I know he will always be good to you, Terrie." Edith gave me one of her wonderful, warm smiles. "I'll miss you terribly if you go to live in Canada, but I love you and if that is what will make you happy, then I'm happy, too."

As we finished our tea, Edith said to me, "Do you remember what I told you when you were a little girl?"

I nodded. I did remember.

"Always follow your dreams. If you think you're right, don't give up your beliefs. Sometimes the obstacles may seem insurmountable, but anything worth having is always worth fighting for, Terrie."

When I left Edith, I felt so much better. I was determined to go to the Investiture and to find a way to convince my parents to allow me to go to London.

I would have to use my clothing coupons wisely if I was to have a new outfit for the Investiture. I shopped carefully and selected a light grey wool suit. The weave had tiny flecks of deep red, so I bought a pretty blouse of the same deep red color. After a long search, I found a small grey hat that matched perfectly. The hat cost more than I wanted to spend, but I couldn't resist buying it. I polished my black leather pumps and carried black kid gloves. The only thing I lacked was a good pair of nylons.

One of the volunteers at the canteen had a nephew who made no secret of the fact that he had connections in the black market. After giving it some thought, I asked her if her nephew could get a pair of nylons for me. A few days later, I tried not to feel guilty as I paid for the nylons. I told myself that I'd resorted to the black market for a very special occasion.

Frank's letter arrived with the date and the time that he'd meet my train in London. He arranged to stay at the hostel. "I've known Gwen since I was in London in 1936," he wrote. "I know you two will get along famously. We'll find a room for you at a hotel near the hostel. Terrie, we'll have two whole days together. I can hardly wait to see you. Give my love to your folks and tell them I'll take very good care of you."

I read his letter over and over. Finally, I took it into the living room where my parents were reading the newspaper.

"Please read this letter from Frank. I think you may feel differently when you see what he has to say."

"Terrie," my father said as he looked up from his paper. "We've already discussed this whole affair and told you our feelings. We do not approve of your going to London with Frank. We're not going to change our minds regardless of his letter. If you go, you will be defying us. Now, we shall hear no more about it."

I'd been confident my parents would change their minds, but I remembered Edith's words and I knew my place was with Frank when he received his medal from the King.

When I asked for two days off work, Mamie said, "Of course, dear. You've worked so many extra hours, you deserve some time off. However, you must promise to tell us every detail of the Investiture when you return."

The day of my journey to London finally arrived. I dressed carefully. I'd used all of my clothing coupons and most of my savings, but I knew it was well worth it. I'd be with Frank in a couple of hours.

As I sat on the train leaving Nottingham, I looked out the window at the beautiful English countryside. I thought of the days before the war and how we could enjoy life without the worry of Germany invading our land. I quickly got that thought out of my head for I knew England would never be beaten. Our stubborn determination would prevail.

When the train stopped at Heathrow Station, I stepped onto the platform and saw Frank waving to me from the gate. I ran to him. When he held me in his arms, I knew I'd made the right decision. I didn't spoil the moment by telling Frank about my parent's attitude. I tried to convince myself that they would change their minds by the time I returned home.

We left the station walking arm in arm, bursting with happiness and anticipation.

"First, we'll go see Gwen. I told her we would be at the hostel by twelve-thirty. I booked a room for you at a small hotel near the hostel. You should be comfortable there. The ceremony takes place at two, so we'll have to be at the palace about one-thirty. After the Investiture, we'll have a nice dinner together."

Frank had everything planned so well, I couldn't help but feel comfortable and safe.

Gwen was waiting at the hostel to greet us. She was quite tall, about forty-five with light brown hair and a warm smile.

"Hello, Terrie," she said. "I feel as if I know you already. Frank has told me so much about you. I'm so proud of Frank. He certainly deserves this award."

Gwen took my arm. "Shall we freshen up a bit before we leave? You look lovely, but after the train ride, I'm sure you want to check your makeup. After all, we're going to Buckingham Palace to see the King." She chuckled. "Who, I realize comes after Frank in your order of importance, I'm sure."

As the three of us sat on the double-decker bus, riding through London, I was shocked to see how much damage enemy bombs had wrought throughout the historic city. London had taken a massive beating—so much rubble everywhere. Some famous landmarks were still standing, though, like St. Paul's Cathedral.

I had to smile when I read the posters some shopkeepers had put up to hide broken store windows. "Jerry was here, but we're open for business as usual," or "Come back in an hour. We're having an air raid."

The London underground served as a shelter for hundreds of British people during the raids. In spite of the terrible loss of lives and property, the people of our tiny island were steadfast in their determination that Hitler and his armies would never set foot on English soil.

When we arrived at Buckingham Palace, I was relieved to see the beautiful building had not been damaged. I was proud as I thought about all of the history that had taken place inside those walls. We walked through the wrought iron gates and Frank gave the guard his papers. We were directed to a waiting room, and a few moments later, Gwen and I were led to an anteroom where we were instructed on the protocol for the occasion. After that, we walked into a large room with five rows of chairs covered with deep red velvet. Portraits of former Kings and Queens of England hung on the walls.

I felt tremendous pride in my country as I was shown to my seat. Gwen gave my hand a tiny squeeze. "Isn't this exciting," she asked. "I can hardly believe it's really happening."

A few minutes later, everyone stood as King George VI entered the room and walked to the podium. The King, of small stature, had a very calm appearance. He wore the dark, navy blue uniform of the British Navy—a double breasted jacket, white shirt and black tie. As we stood to sing the national anthem, my eyes filled with tears of pride and happiness.

One by one, servicemen walked up to the ramp to stand in front of the King. The King stood tall and greeted each serviceman with a warm smile and a handshake. He was known to have a speech impediment, but he did well that day as he spoke a few words before he pinned a medal on each man's jacket.

I could see Frank walking behind a young redheaded airman who was on crutches. His left pant leg was pinned up to the knee. My heart was in my mouth as I watched the airman climb the ramp, face the king and then walk down the ramp to his seat. A grin lit up his boyish face. I hoped his parents were in the audience. How proud they must have been of their young son.

When Frank stood in front of the King, I knew I'd never forget that moment. I hoped Frank and I would have children so we could tell them about it. After receiving his medal, Frank's eyes sought mine and he gave me a big smile.

Gwen and I waited for Frank in the courtyard at the palace where reporters were interviewing the servicemen and taking pictures for the newspaper.

"Where are you from," they asked Frank. "What are your plans for after the war?"

"Well, first let's get the war over," Frank said. "My home is in Winnipeg, Canada, but I doubt if I'll stay there in peacetime. I'm going to build a sailboat and live closer to the ocean with this little English girl I plan to marry."

I couldn't stop blushing as the reporters took pictures of Frank and me together. I was so happy I could hardly answer when the reporters asked where my home was. I knew the Nottingham papers would probably have an article and my parents would not be happy to see my name and picture.

After an early dinner, Gwen said, "Well, Frank, it's been a wonderful day, but since all good things do end, I must get back to the hostel. I'll see you later tonight. Terrie, I enjoyed meeting you so much. If you have the chance to come to London again, please look me up. I'll always be glad to see you.

Frank and I walked for a while and talked about our future.

Then, Frank said, "It's been a wonderful day, but a long one for both of us. I'd better take you to your hotel."

The hotel was nice. I took the noisy three-passenger lift up to my room on the 4th floor. My room had just enough space for the single bed, a dresser, chair, and a bedside table with a lamp. The one window had a heavy blackout curtain that reached to the brown carpeted floor.

Frank and I sat together on the bed. He held me in his arms. "Terrie, I love you so much. I'd like to stay and make love with you. But I know we must resist the temptation."

I felt such a strange emotion at that moment. I wasn't sure whether I was happy or disappointed.

"I'm going to Wales early tomorrow to go to school and I have no idea when we'll be together again."

I snuggled close to him and said, "Frank, I love you and I'm grateful for your patience. I want you to stay with me, but I know it would be wrong."

We kissed goodnight, the both of us struggling to keep our love in control. I didn't sleep well that night. I knew many months would pass before Frank and I would be together again.

The following morning, Frank picked me up and after a long walk, we had breakfast in a coffee shop near the station. Our trains took different directions, Frank's to Wales and mine to Nottingham. As I boarded the train, I wondered how I could be so happy and sad at once. I would never forget the Investiture, but when would I see Frank again?

I walked home from the station to tell my family about King George VI and Buckingham Palace and the wonderful experience I had been a part of.

I could hear Kathleen's voice as I opened the front door. I rushed into the living room. "Hello, everyone. I'm home."

All I received were glares from Mom, Dad and Billy. I dropped my suitcase beside an empty chair and said, in a breathless voice, "I'm so glad you're all here. I can hardly wait to tell you about the Investiture. It was so exciting."

Complete silence filled the room. At last, Billy spoke. "Well, Terrie, I hope you're satisfied. Mother and Dad are really angry with you and I don't blame them. You deliberately defied them by going to London and spending the night with Frank."

I was stunned by his outburst. I took a moment to regain my composure. "You're not being fair. Frank and I did nothing wrong. I told you before I left that he would be staying at a hostel and I would stay in a hotel. That's exactly what happened. You should all be proud to know him, and happy that I had such a wonderful experience."

Dad looked at me. "Terrie, you made your choice. We asked you not to go to London, but you went anyway. We do not want to discuss this any further. Frank is no longer welcome in this house and we forbid you to have anything more to do with him. That is final!"

I couldn't respond. I ran from the room to my bedroom upstairs and laid on my bed, crying. There was a tap on the door.

"May I come in?" Marjorie put her arms around me and said, "I really don't understand your parents' attitude, but I can't interfere, Terrie. Even though Bill is my husband, I think he's behaving very foolishly. One day he'll realize how unfair he was. Your mother made such a terrible fuss that I think your dad and Bill are just trying to keep the peace. You did the right thing by going to Frank." Then, Marjorie said, "Now, I want to hear all about your trip."

I was so grateful for my sister-in-law's friendship. "What hurts most," I told her, "is the lack of confidence Mom and Dad have in Frank and me. We had every opportunity to spend the night together, but we knew we would wait until we were married. They should respect Frank for that."

At work the next morning, the whole staff was waiting for me to tell them about the Investiture. Thank goodness for my many friends at the Y. They all thought so highly of Frank.

I worked very hard the next few days to keep my mind off my loneliness. To help, I went to visit Edith. I told her about the problem at home.

"Well, dear, you did nothing to be ashamed of. Just try to be patient. Your family will reconsider when they have a chance to see how foolish they are being. The real problem is that your mother is afraid Frank will take you away from her. Kathleen has a boyfriend, and Bill and Marjorie will soon find a place of their own. I think she's worried about being left alone."

"But she won't be alone. She has Daddy. Besides, Frank and I can't be married until after the war's over and Mother must know I can't leave England in wartime."

Things did not improve at home. I was more lonely and unhappy than I'd ever been. I didn't hear from Frank for some time and my parents continued to be cool toward me. I turned to Edith and the Y for consolation.

One afternoon, my sister Kathleen came home for a visit. I was getting tea ready for the family when she came into the kitchen. "Well, Terrie, you certainly made a mess of things by going to London. I don't blame Mom and Dad for getting upset. You went against their wishes to be with that Canadian who's probably just another serviceman who'll forget you ever existed as soon as he goes home."

"That's not true," I said, angrier than I'd ever been in my life. "We plan to be married one day."

"That's a laugh. You're too young to be married without Mom and Dad's consent. How do you plan to get to Canada"?

Kathleen continued before I had time to answer. "Oh, by the way, Phil asked me to marry him. Mother and Dad are delighted. They told me I can start to make arrangements for a nice wedding." Kathleen flipped her hair and left the kitchen, almost bumping into Billy on the way.

"Now, I want the truth," he yelled. "Did you spend the night with that airman?"

"I've already told everyone that I did not. Why do you keep questioning me?"

"Because I know what men are like and Frank is no different. If you're pregnant, I'll personally beat the tar out of him."

I stood there, stunned. I could feel my face getting flushed as I stared at my brother. "How dare you talk to me that way," I said. "Who do you think you are to accuse me of such things? Frank is twice the man you are and I would certainly not talk about beating him up. He's too much of a gentleman to start a fight, but if you did, he'd be the one to finish it."

I left Billy standing alone in the middle of the kitchen.

The days at home became more unpleasant. I knew I wouldn't be able to stand being at home much longer. I'd have to find a place to live. I told Marjorie my plans.

"I cannot stand being treated this way. If I can find a place I can afford, I'm going to move out."

Marjorie hugged me. "I wish I could help you. Maybe one

of your girlfriends will share a place with you. If you leave, I want you to promise to keep in touch with me."

The following morning, I approached Mamie with my request. "May I rent a room in your house?"

"Well, dear, I would love to have you, but Mom and Dad are living with me. I just don't have any room. Why don't you ask Madge. She'd probably love company now that her husband is overseas."

When I approached Madge, her eyes lit up. "Oh, Terrie, that would be perfect. I hate being in the house alone. I have a spare room and we can share the kitchen. I know we'll get along just fine."

We decided on a rent figure that I could afford, so the arrangements were settled. That evening, I told Marjorie I was moving.

"I'm sorry to see this happen, but I understand how you feel. Your folks are both home now. Why don't you try to reason with them one more time?"

I gave Marjorie a hug. "Thank you for being so good to me. You're truly my sister."

My parents were in the living room. As I looked at them, my heart felt heavy. I loved them and didn't want to hurt them, but I was not willing to give Frank up just to please them.

"I'd like to speak to you both. Please listen to me."

Dad looked up from his paper. "Terrie, if it's about your relationship with Frank, there's nothing more to discuss. You know our feelings and we haven't changed them. If you'll forget him, we'll try to forget about your escapade in London."

At that moment, I knew I had to make a choice.

"Apparently, you don't trust me. I love Frank and he has

asked me to marry him when the war is over. I cannot continue to live here with my whole family ignoring or insulting me. I've done nothing to deserve this treatment, so I'm leaving and moving in with a girlfriend. I love you both very much and one day I hope to prove to you that I'm making the right decision."

With tears running down my cheeks, I ran from the room. I put a few things in a suitcase and walked out of the house to the bus stop.

My world was changing. I didn't like it.

Madge lived a few miles from the Y. She opened the front door and welcomed me with a hug. I felt lonely as I sat in the cozy little bedroom in Madge's home.

At long last, I received a letter from Frank giving me his new address. He had completed 35 missions over Germany and Italy, and two complete tours of active duty. Now, he had been accepted for pilot training. He wrote that he was very busy with his studies, and sent his love to my family. He was due for a weekend leave very soon and would let me know when he'd be in Nottingham.

When I wrote back to him, I asked him to send all future mail to me at the Y. I didn't want to worry him, so I explained I'd get his letters faster if he sent them to me at work.

After hearing from Frank, I felt more settled into my new life. Madge and I spent time together and enjoyed each other's company. I was almost nineteen, with lots of energy. I began to smile more and to feel a real happiness at work, which I hadn't for a long time. I still loved to dance and practiced regularly in Madge's small living room. I remembered my promise to Edith and knew my dancing would be an asset for me one day.

When I received Frank's letter telling me he'd be in

Nottingham on leave in two weeks, I could hardly wait to see him. The time seemed so long since my trip to London. So much had happened in the two months since then.

After what seemed an endless wait, the big day arrived. I waited on the platform at Victoria Station for Frank's train. The train was on time and I spotted Frank almost immediately, dodging people as he ran down the crowded platform. When Frank held me in his arms, I wanted to stay there forever. I felt so secure. All of the problems of the past months seemed to fade away as we kissed.

"Frank, I've missed you so much. I can't believe you're really here."

"I've missed you, too, honey. I wish I could be with you for more than a weekend, but I guess we must be thankful for the time we have together while this damn war is on. Now that the Yanks are helping, Hitler will soon be beaten. Come on. . .let's go see your folks. I'm going to ask their permission to marry you."

"Could we go somewhere for a cup of tea, first?" I wondered how I was going to tell him about what had happened. We found a small English tearoom, with little tables covered in white tablecloths and napkins, china cups and saucers and plates, silver teaspoons, and a sugar bowl and cream jug in matching china. A waitress pushed a trolley cart to our table with a variety of scones. She wore a black uniform with a starched white apron.

As we sat in the little tearoom, I took a deep breath and told Frank about my parents' attitude. I didn't mention Billy's accusations or my sister's remarks. I did tell him, though, how supportive Marjorie and Edith had been.

"I don't understand their attitude," Frank said, "but I think we have to straighten things out at once. Come on, let's go see them. I'm sure I can get things right. They probably think we want to marry at once. I'll let them know that we'll wait for the war to end."

Marjorie answered the phone. "Your mother is here, but your dad isn't home from work, yet. He should be here any time. Are you coming to see us?"

I was nervous as Frank and I walked to Sherwood. When we were near the house, I took Frank's hand. "No matter what the outcome is, I want to be your wife."

"Don't worry, honey, I'll explain everything and get approval from your folks. We'll be married as soon as we can and one day we'll build that sailboat. I want a family. We have so much to do that we have to be together a thousand years in order to get everything done."

The front door was not locked, but I felt like a stranger. I knocked on the door. Marjorie answered and greeted me with a hug. "I've missed you, dear. You both look wonderful. Congratulations on your pilot training, Frank. Bill's in the living room with your mother, Terrie, but your dad isn't home yet."

"Hello, Mom," I said as we entered the room. "Frank has leave for the weekend and he'd like to talk to you and Dad."

Bill stood. "Terrie, I thought Mom and Dad made it quite clear that Frank is not welcome here."

"How can you be so rude, Bill? Frank's not here to talk to you. He wants to talk to Mom and Dad."

Frank spoke up. "I don't want to seem disrespectful, but I really don't know what the problem is. Terrie and I love each other and I would like permission to marry her after the war."

The door opened and my dad came into the room. "I heard what you said, Frank. I will never give my consent for our

daughter to marry a serviceman from a country on the other side
of the world. You're much older than Terrie and you destroyed
our trust in you by encouraging her to stay in London with you.
Terrie is welcome to live at home, but she must discontinue her
relationship with you right now."

Frank took a deep breath. "I'm sorry you can't see what a
happy future Terrie and I could have together. I'll be going back
to Wales tomorrow to get my orders for an assignment overseas.
It worries me to leave Terrie here when she is being made so
unhappy. We've done nothing wrong and you're being very
unfair to her."

I was shocked. Frank had not told me about his next
assignment. I felt a chill in my heart when I thought of being
without him.

My parents looked at us. Dad finally spoke. "Frank, we
wish you good luck with your flying. Terrie is making problems
for herself. She knows she's welcome to come home, but we'll not
approve of her relationship with you."

As we left, Marjorie was crying. "Frank, Terrie can always
come to me. Don't worry, one day the family will realize how
wrong they are."

When we walked back to Sherwood to catch a bus, neither
Frank nor I spoke for some time. Finally, I said, "You didn't tell
me this was your last leave before you go overseas."

Frank stopped and turned to look at me. "I didn't want to
spoil the time we have together. I was going to tell you tomorrow
before I go back. I've finished my ground training and I'm being
sent to Montreal for flight school. When I get my wings, I'll
probably be sent to the Pacific."

I shuddered. How could that be?

"Try not to be upset. I love you and as soon as possible, I'm going to marry you. I'll never let you go and I'll never forget you. Be patient. Things will work out, eventually. Come on, let's go for dinner and enjoy the rest of our time together."

Frank slept on the couch at Madge's house. The next morning, as the three of us enjoyed breakfast in the tiny kitchen, Madge told Frank how upset everyone at the Y was at the way my family was treating me. "We'll take good care of her, Frank, so don't worry."

We went to Victoria Station where Frank would catch the train to Wales. I wondered if I'd ever see him again. I quickly put the thought out of my mind. I decided that I had to adopt a positive attitude. Frank was so sure of our future together. As I walked back to Madge's little house, I concentrated on plans for after the war when Frank and I would be together.

I made a mental note to buy a book about Canada and learn about the country that would be my home someday.

Chapter 4

The days were long, but letters from Frank arrived regularly. He was enjoying flight training. One morning I arrived at the Y to find a small package waiting for me. I was excited as I opened it. Inside I found a tiny heart-shaped box that contained a gold ring, set with a small diamond. Tears filled my eyes as I read the note inside the box. "Please remember this ring means you are mine forever."

I hurried to where Mamie was talking with Jim Edgar. "Look what was in the package."

"May I have the honor of putting the ring on your finger in Frank's place?" Jim said.

"My hands are shaking so badly, you may have a problem, but please try." I could hardly wait to show Mom and Dad. Surely they'd approve after they saw the ring. They'd no longer have doubts about Frank's intentions.

I had another surprise that day. Later in the afternoon, I was working at the registration desk when one of the voluntary helpers told me a serviceman was asking for me. My heart leapt. Had Frank somehow managed to get back to England?

I hurried to the canteen where the serviceman was waiting. There I saw a tall, handsome soldier wearing the kilt of the Canadian Scottish Highlanders.

"I'm Captain Charlie Jardine," he announced. "I'm Frank's brother-in-law. Come here so I can give you an official welcome to the family."

After his bear hug, I said, "Let's go into the office. I want to hear all about the family. Which of Frank's sisters are you married to? What is Winnipeg like? Where are you stationed?"

"Hold on there. It'll take a while to answer all those questions. Let's find a place to have a drink and talk."

Mamie agreed to let me have a few hours off. "Go ahead, don't hurry. You deserve some free time."

Charlie and I went to a local pub where I ordered ginger ale and gave Charlie my liquor rations. Charlie seemed happy to be able to order an extra Scotch.

Charlie told me he was married to Dorothy, the youngest of Frank's sisters. She was six years older than Frank. Their little son, Tony, was a year old. Charlie had been shipped overseas before Tony was born, so he'd never seen his little boy. "All I have are pictures of him. He doesn't even know his daddy."

How sad. War caused all kinds of separations within families.

"The Dagg's are a swell family. Their mother and father died when Frank was three. Frank was taken care of by his brothers and sisters. There are six girls—Maude, Lydia,

Marguerite and Dorothy, who all live in Winnipeg. May and Ruth are in Vancouver. An older sister, Laura, died at birth. The four brothers are Roy, Albert, Chauncey and Frank. Roy and Albert live in Winnipeg. Chauncey, who is four years older than Frank, lives in Vancouver. And Frank is the youngest of all."

I was beginning to feel overwhelmed.

"When we get together," Charlie continues, "it's quite a gang. They'll make you feel very welcome, Terrie. I know how happy they are that their young brother is ready to settle down with his little English bride when the war is over."

I told Charlie about how my parents objected to my relationship with Frank.

"Well, maybe I can do something to change their minds. Can we go see them? I'll tell them about the family and surely, when they see your ring, they'll know Frank's intentions are sincere."

I was willing to try. I'd do anything to have my family's blessing.

"Okay, let's go. There's no time like the present. Lead on McDuff," Charlie said.

My heart was light as we took the bus to Sherwood. Charlie was confident that things would be better after he talked to my parents. But, when Charlie and I arrived at the house, things didn't turn out as I'd hoped. Marjorie opened the door and held her arms out to me. "Hello, dear."

"Marjorie, this is Captain Jardine. He's Frank's brother-in-law. He wants to talk to Mom and Dad, and I want you to be the first of the family to see my ring."

Marjorie took my hand.

"It's lovely. You know I wish all the very best for you and

Frank. Your folks are having tea. Kathleen's with them."

I led Charlie into the living room. "Hello, everyone. I want you to meet Captain Jardine, Frank's brother-in-law. He's stationed close by, and he wanted to meet my family."

Dad stood as Charlie went forward to shake his hand. "We're glad to meet you, Captain. However, if you're here to discuss the relationship between Frank and our daughter, I want you to know the matter is closed. We've already given Terrie our decision and we have not changed our minds."

I was embarrassed that Dad would be so rude. But, I had to speak. "Daddy, I came to show you my ring. I received it today." As I approached, Mother said, "Teresa, we are aware that Frank has sent you a ring. We received a letter from him asking for our consent to your engagement. We didn't reply because we thought we made it quite clear to both of you that we will never consent to your marriage to a foreigner."

"Now, just a minute, Mrs. Allen," Charlie said. "I'm also a Canadian and we do not consider ourselves foreigners. We're here fighting for your country and mine. You should be proud to have Frank propose to your daughter. He's a fine man and he comes from a swell family. It seems to me you're being unfair to deny these two young people their chance for happiness."

"Captain, you're upsetting my wife." Dad said. "I would be obliged if you would leave. We're planning a wedding for Kathleen and her fiancé, and we do not need this unpleasantness. Terrie cannot marry without our consent for at least two years. By that time, Frank will have forgotten her and she will have found an acceptable Englishman to marry."

Kathleen finally spoke. "When we were children, Terrie, I planned that we'd be each other's bridesmaids when we married.

But, Terrie, you've caused so much upset in the family, it's now impossible for you to be in my wedding party. Why don't you forget that Canadian. I'm sure he won't wait for you."

I turned to walk out of the room, but before I left, I looked back at my family. "Frank's family has accepted me without even meeting me. Frank was made welcome here until he asked me to marry him. I don't understand, but I know you'll never change your minds. Kathleen, I wish you and Phil every happiness."

Marjorie ran to me as Charlie opened the front door to leave. "I'll always be here if you need me. Give my love to Frank when you write. I'm delighted to have met you, Charlie."

I was silent as we walked to the bus stop. I had a lump in my throat, and my mind was a million miles away.

Charlie put his arm around me. "Well, Honey, all you can do now is wait. Maybe they'll feel differently when we finally end this war."

"I don't intend to wait, Charlie. I've made up my mind. Frank won't be sent back to England, so I'm going to Canada."

"I can't say I blame you for wanting to do just that. But isn't that impossible? There's no way they'll allow a civilian to leave England. It's wartime."

"I'm going to find a way, Charlie. I want to be with Frank."

Before leaving me at Madge's house, Charlie gave me a hug. "Frank is a lucky guy to have you to love him. I don't know what you have in mind, but you have my address and telephone number. Call if you need me."

That night, I wrote to the Canadian Consulate in London. I told him I was engaged to Frank and we wanted to be married. I asked if there was any possibility of my getting passage to Canada. I gave Frank's name, rank and serial number. As I put the letter in the postbox the following morning, I said a silent prayer that my request would not be ignored.

And it wasn't. My prayer was answered. A few weeks later, I received a reply from the Consulate telling me I must have a statement signed by Frank's commanding officer giving Frank permission to marry me.

I wrote Frank immediately, asking him to get the necessary papers to me as soon as possible.

Several weeks passed before I received a letter from Frank with the papers signed by his commanding officer. In his letter, Frank wrote, "I feel so helpless. There is really nothing I can do from here. I never received a reply to my letter from your parents, so I realize they still do not approve of our marriage. I'm sorry you are going against their wishes. They are giving you no choice."

I knew the next step would be difficult. I had to arrange a court hearing to get permission from a magistrate to marry because I was under twenty-one. I made the application at the courthouse. Then, a few days later, when I received notice of the date and time for the hearing, my heart sank. My parents were ordered to appear. I called Charlie to ask if he would go to court with me to represent Frank. Charlie agreed immediately and told me to just let him know when I needed him.

I slept fitfully the night before the hearing. I joined Madge for breakfast. I wore the suit I'd worn for Frank's Investiture.

"This will be a hard day for you, Terrie," Madge said. "But, it will soon be over and I'm sure things will go well for you. You know I wish you the best of luck."

"Thank you, Madge. I just wish it didn't have to be this way. I love Frank and I know this is the only way we'll have a future together."

Charlie was waiting for me when I arrived at the Y. "You look great, honey. You're a brave girl and have the courage of your convictions. Keep your chin up and remember I'm with you all the way."

When Charlie and I arrived at the courthouse, we were directed to a small courtroom and shown to our seats. My heart was in my throat when I saw my father seated across the room. Bill was with him. Neither of them acknowledged me. Again, I felt like a stranger in the presence of my family.

The judge was an elderly man. He had a kind face, but it was expressionless as he sat down and the proceedings began.

I was asked to stand and explain my reasons for being there. I was confident as I told the judge my story. I explained how Frank had completed two tours of operations in England and now was finishing pilot training and would probably be sent to the Pacific. "He has permission from his commanding officer to be married, but I need your consent because my parents will not agree to our marriage."

Next, Charlie was asked his relationship to the case. "Well, your Honor, my brother-in-law is unable to be here to represent himself. He is now retraining in Canada after flying 35 missions. I wanted to speak for him. I feel that he and Terrie should have their chance at happiness. Frank is a fine man and comes from a wonderful family who will welcome Terrie as a member."

My heart pounded as my father stood to speak.

"Terrie has upset our family with this nonsense. Her mother would not come today because she feels Terrie is being very foolish. We both know this is just another wartime romance. We have told our daughter she is welcome to come home when she discontinues her relationship with Frank Dagg."

Bill was not asked to speak. I knew he was probably disappointed because he scowled at me throughout the entire proceedings. After what seemed an eternity, I was asked to stand in front of the judge.

"Well, young lady, I have listened to both sides in this disagreement, and I believe you and your fiancé should have your chance to be together. Your parents seem to be making life pretty unhappy for you. I doubt that you'll be able to marry for a while since it will not be possible for you to leave England until the war is over. However, you have the court's permission to marry. I would like to offer my personal good wishes to both of you. May you have a long and happy life together."

I wanted to throw my arms around the judge as he smiled at me. I could feel the tears forming as I thanked him. When I turned to Charlie, I noticed my father and brother had already left the courtroom.

"Charlie, now I know how it feels to be happy and sad at the same time. Do you think my family will ever forgive me?"

"Of course they will, honey. Remember, though, they're the same stubborn Britishers who are winning this war. I have to get back to camp now or we could celebrate. I'll be in touch. Write Frank at once with the news. Tell him I said 'Hi'."

"How can I ever thank you, Charlie. You've been so good to me."

"Just invite me to the wedding," Charlie said as he ran to catch the bus.

I went at once to tell Edith the news. The sweet old lady was so happy to see me. "Don't worry, dear, your family will come around. They should know you by now. Once you make up your mind, you follow through. That's a good quality. Terrie, your determination will always keep you strong in life's challenges."

My friends at the Y were pleased with the outcome of the hearing. Their support gave me the extra confidence I needed to face the next challenge.

I wrote to Frank to tell him the results of the court hearing and then I wrote a letter to the Consulate enclosing the necessary documents. Now all I could do was wait.

Work kept me very busy. The days still seemed endless as I waited for a reply from the Canadian consulate. Finally, I received a very official looking brown manila envelope sealed with red wax. I mustered all my courage to break the seal. I opened the document and read that I had been granted passage on a ship that would leave England from Prestwick, Scotland. I was instructed to send 29 pounds, more than I earned in two weeks, immediately to a Captain Gill at a military address. The letter said he must receive it right away and I would then be notified as to the time and date of my departure. I was warned not to tell anyone the contents of the letter due to wartime security.

I was so excited that it took me a few minutes to realize I had another big obstacle to overcome. I didn't have the money and had no idea how I could raise 29 pounds. There was no way Frank could get it to me in time and I couldn't tell anyone why I needed the money.

I was preoccupied as I hurried to work that evening. I noticed the darkness in the reception hall and wondered who had forgotten to turn on the lights. The hall was a popular place for the servicemen to gather. Usually the lights were lit late into the night. I walked in to turn on the lights, but as I reached for the switch, the room suddenly lit up and I was greeted with, "Surprise. Surprise."

I thought I must be dreaming. The young men of the youth club, the canteen and office staff, and many of the volunteers filled the room. Jim Edgar came forward and took my arm. "Terrie, we decided that since we don't know when you and Frank will be married, we'd offer our congratulations in the form of a party. May I please have the first dance with you?"

The evening was wonderful. Everyone enjoyed dancing to the music of gramophone records. They played all the popular recordings of the Dorsey brothers and Glenn Miller. It was hard to imagine a war still had to be won because the celebration was so gay. Toward the end of the evening, Jim Edgar stepped to the middle of the room. "Please be quiet everyone," he said. "Terrie, will you join me? I have an announcement to make."

I stood beside Jim, surrounded by my friends. He took my hand.

"A few years ago, a little girl of almost sixteen came to me looking for a job. She thought she had fooled me into believing she was eighteen. She seemed so earnest and anxious to work that I decided to take a chance and hire her. We have never regretted that decision as Terrie has proved to be a hard worker and a popular member of our staff. She has done a great deal to make the Y a pleasant place for the servicemen. We want you and Frank to know that you have the very best wishes of everyone here."

Jim handed me an envelope, saying, "This is from all of us."

I reached up to give him a kiss and to thank him. Then, Kenny Williams, a member of the youth's club, came up to me. "You're marrying the best chess player we ever had in the club. We'd like you and Frank to have this little gift from all the boy's club members."

Kenny's face turned red as I gave him a hug. He hurried back to his buddies as one of the volunteers walked to my side.

"We all enjoy working in the canteen with you. We want to wish you and Frank many years of happiness together. We all hope it will not be too long until you can be married."

She handed me another envelope. The lump in my throat made it difficult to talk. When I found my voice, I looked at all the familiar faces and said, "I don't know when we'll be able to be married. I can't tell you how much your support has meant to me. Frank and I will remember you all with much love and we'll keep in touch. Thank you all, again."

Mamie and Madge ran to hug me. "We planned this party a week ago. Don't you think we did a good job keeping it a secret?"

I smiled. If only they knew what big secret I was keeping from them.

That night, when Madge and I arrived home, we made tea and I opened the three envelopes. I found three checks. The total was more than enough for my passage. I would even have enough money for the train fare from New York to Winnipeg. I longed to tell Madge the news, but I knew I couldn't.

"I'll put the checks into the bank until I need the money. It'll be a wonderful nest egg to start our marriage. I can never thank you enough, Madge, for letting me stay here."

The following morning, I mailed the money to Captain Gill. I called Marjorie and asked her to meet me at Edith's apartment the following Saturday.

"Is anything wrong, dear?"

"No, I have important news and I need to see you."

When Marjorie arrived at Edith's, I told them about the party the Y members gave me. "I'll be leaving England soon, but I'm sworn to secrecy so I can't tell you exactly when. I'll miss everyone here. I was hoping to see Mom and Dad before I go. Please don't mention this to anyone."

Edith had tears in her eyes when she spoke. "Terrie, I've loved you since the day your mother let me hold you when you were a tiny baby. You are really all I have in the world and I want your happiness. I know this means you're leaving to be with Frank. I've always told you to follow your dreams, but I want a promise from you before you leave. You must assure me that you'll keep up your dancing. I have a feeling it will be important to you one day."

Marjorie was quiet. When she spoke, she sounded sad. "I don't think your parents will see you, Terrie. Your mother is very bitter. I really believe your dad would give in, but he has to keep peace with your mother. I have to live with Bill." She shrugged. "I've told him he'll regret his actions one day. They're wrong in hurting you instead of helping you. Kathleen and Phil are planning their wedding this month. The reception will be held at the Victoria Hotel right opposite the Y. I know how hard it'll be for you to be excluded. You can try calling, but I think your parents will reject you." Marjorie handed me a package. "This is for you both, from Bill and me. I hope you'll forgive your brother one day."

I opened the gift to find a beautiful carving set with bone handles. The three pieces were in a black box lined with velour.

"It's beautiful and the first present we have for our home. We'll treasure it always." I hugged Marjorie. "You're the best sister a girl ever had. I'll miss you terribly."

"I'll come to see Edith often," Marjorie promised, as she turned to leave. "You take care of yourself, Terrie, and write when you can. Give my love to Frank."

I turned to Edith. "I have to go to work, but I'll see you again very soon. I'll miss you more than anyone. Promise me you'll take good care of yourself. Frank and I will come to

England for a visit as soon as we can."

Two days later, I received the letter with my tickets and
instructions. I was to be in Scotland in less than a week. I sent
a wire to Frank telling him of my arrival time in Winnipeg.
The ship would dock in New York, then I'd go by train, first to
Montreal, then Winnipeg. If all connections went as scheduled,
the journey would take nine days. I decided to stay at the Y the
night before I left, because the train to Scotland departed Victoria
Station very early.

Madge's husband, George, was home on leave and I told
them I thought it would be nice for them to have the house to
themselves. Madge accepted this reason for my staying at the Y
on my last night in Nottingham.

"You don't have to do that," Madge said, "but we do
appreciate your thoughtfulness."

The next morning, I called Charlie.

"Is anything wrong, honey?" he said.

"No, Charlie. I may be leaving soon and I want to see you."
We arranged to meet for lunch. Charlie knew that I must not
mention dates so he asked no questions when we met.

"Please give Dorothy a big hug for me," Charlie said. "Tell
her I love her and can hardly wait to see her and Tony."

As I watched Charlie board the bus, I wondered how long it
would be before I'd see him again.

I tried to call my family. Kathleen answered the phone.
"Terrie, I think I can speak for Mother and Dad. You've upset the
whole family with your foolishness. Phil and I had a beautiful
wedding and it gave Mother so much pleasure, I hate to see her
upset again by your call. What do you want, anyway?"

I tried to keep my cool as I said, "Kathleen, I may be leaving
England and I would like another chance to make things right.

Would you please have one of them come to the phone?"

After a pause, Kathleen said, "I can't believe you're being so stubborn. There's no way you can leave England until after the war. Getting permission to be married the way you did was a terrible blow to Mom and Dad. Why don't you leave well enough alone."

I pleaded one more time for Kathleen to ask one of my parents to come to the phone. After what seemed an eternity, I was disappointed once again to hear Kathleen's voice. "Mother says that she'll be happy to talk to you if you decide to give up this ridiculous thing with that Canadian."

By now, I was weary. "Kathleen, I do hope you and Phil will have a wonderful life together. I'm sorry you can't be more understanding about Frank and me. Maybe one day you'll change your thinking. I can't say when I'll be leaving England, but please tell Mother and Dad I'll contact them as soon as I can."

I hung up and thought my heart would break. I went to see Edith. "Oh, Edith, I'm so torn. I want to be with Frank so much, but I don't want to leave without making peace with Mom and Dad."

"I wish there was something I could do," Edith said. "You mustn't feel too badly. You have done all you can to try to make things right. Now you must follow your dream and go to Frank. When you're happily married, your parents will realize they were wrong. I know you can't tell me when you're going, but please promise to let me know as soon as you are safely with Frank."

Edith gave me a hug and handed me a package. I opened it to find a beautiful sewing basket fitted with needles, scissors and spools of thread. As I thanked her with a kiss, I wondered if I would ever see my old nurse again. Edith was almost 80 years old. This wonderfully wise and unselfish woman had devoted much of her life to me. I knew I would never forget the promises I had made and would remember everything Edith had taught me for the rest of my life.

Chapter 5

I was unable to sleep on the eve of my departure. I had
packed my few belongings in a steamer trunk and taken it to the
station the day before I left to arrange for its shipment to the dock
in Scotland.

As I left the Y for the last time, it took all the courage I could
muster not to look back. I stood on the deserted platform at
Victoria Station for the second time in fourteen months. Strangely,
I wasn't nervous. I had confidence that I was doing the right
thing. As dawn began to break, I wondered what lay ahead for
me. I was leaving everything I loved to go to a strange land,
a new family and a man I had not seen for fourteen months. I
chased all the thoughts away as I promised myself I would get
home to see my family once Frank and I married and the war was
ended.

I was not concerned about crossing an ocean where German mines and submarines still lurked ready to attack our allied ships. I just knew I would soon be with Frank.

When I boarded the train bound for Scotland, I felt filled with anxiety and loneliness.

When the train arrived in Prestwick, I asked the station master if he could tell me where I could find a room for the night.

"Try the YWCA," he told me. "It's very close to the station and I'm sure they would have a room for you. It's inexpensive, too."

I walked the short distance to the YWCA and asked the desk clerk for a room. "How long will you be staying?" The middle-aged lady said.

"Just overnight."

"We have one vacant room on the second floor. The bath is at the end of the hall. I'll have someone show you to it."

I paid the clerk and followed a young girl upstairs to a small, clean room. "Is there any where I can get dinner close by?"

"Well, a light supper is served in the dining room at seven and you're welcome to join us," the clerk said.

After I took a relaxing bath and dressed, I felt much better. In the dining room I sat at a table with three girls and managed to avoid telling them the real reason for my visit to Scotland. I said I was visiting friends the next day. After saying goodnight, I went to my room and tried to sleep. I kept thinking about my family, and the uncertainty that lay ahead. I couldn't help wondering what would be waiting for me in Prestwick harbor the next morning.

I was awake and dressed long before necessary. I walked the short distance to the dock, but when I arrived I could hardly

believe what I saw—The Queen Mary! She had now become
a troop ship. I was stunned. Even in her wartime attire, the
beautiful ship was elegant. Her staterooms had been turned into
dorm-like accommodations. About 600 servicemen were aboard,
many of them wounded GI's going home to America.

A steward directed me to a cabin on the lower deck. I'd be
sharing the small quarters with three other girls. There were two
sets of upper and lower bunks. Since I was the last one to arrive,
I took a top bunk. Two of my roommates were English girls who
were joining their husbands. The third was a friendly Canadian
girl.

The Canadian girl was Norma Blake and I felt comfortable
with her at once. Norma told me she was on her way to Montreal
to join her family. Her husband, an English flyer, had been killed
on a mission a few months earlier.

The sea voyage was wonderful. The Atlantic Ocean was
calm and the sun shown brightly on the seas. It was like a dream.
I had always loved the water and found myself thinking of the
boat Frank and I would build one day. I found it hard to imagine
a war was still raging in Europe as the magnificent Queen Mary
gently sailed toward America.

The days at sea went quickly. The troops were entertained
by Fred Astaire's wonderful dancing and Bing Crosby's singing.
The four of us were able to enjoy their fabulous entertainment,
too. I could tell the servicemen were happy to be headed home, so
the journey went well.

I had a lump in my throat when I saw the Statue of Liberty
as we sailed into New York harbor and watched the GI's cheer and
salute the lady. I thought of the hundreds of people who'd been
welcomed to American shores through the years. Now, I knew

how the immigrants must have felt who had come from other countries in turmoil to start a new life in a new world. There were few dry eyes aboard the ship as someone began to sing America's National Anthem. I was sure many of the GI's aboard the Queen Mary had wondered if they would ever set foot on American soil again.

I'll never forget that morning.

I was sorry to leave that beautiful ship. The journey had been so peaceful, and I'd been able to clear my mind. I was prepared to continue the rest of my long journey.

Norma and I passed through customs together. Our papers were in order and I arranged for my trunk to be sent to Winnipeg. I had a small overnight case that I carried with me.

The two of us boarded the train to Montreal. During our trip, Norma invited me to spend a few hours at her parent's home. "You'll have time between trains and I know Dad will be happy to drive you back to the station."

I accepted the invitation, gladly. I'd become fond of my new friend.

We arrived in Montreal where Norma had a tearful reunion with her parents. Norma resembled her mother, a pretty dark-haired woman. Her father, a tall, handsome man had a welcoming smile.

"We'd love to have you visit us," Mrs. Blake said. "It'll be no problem to get you back to the station to catch your train to Winnipeg."

Montreal was a cosmopolitan city. The beautiful buildings and shops fascinated me as we passed them on the drive to Norma's home.

The Blake's made me feel welcome. I couldn't help noticing the closeness of that family, compared with mine back in England.

The time flew by and it seemed only minutes until I had to return to the station. When I thanked Mrs. Blake, the older woman put her arms around me and said, "We're so happy to have Norma home, but we wish the circumstances could be different. We adored our son-in-law. Even though they lived far away, we were happy knowing they had such a good life together. I hope Norma will marry again one day. She's too young to be alone."

I found saying goodbye to Norma's family hard to do. The Blake's had known me for such a very short time, yet I felt very close to them.

The train to Winnipeg was different from the trains in England. When I boarded the train the porter had already made up the berths so I soon climbed into my narrow, curtained bunk and slept like a baby to the clickety-clacking of the wheels. I awoke early and opened the drapes, looking up and down the corridor. All was quiet so I slipped to the carpeted aisle and made my way to the ladies restroom. I found the restroom occupied by a lady who appeared to be in her early fifties.

"I don't sleep well on trains," the lady said. "You sound English. Are you?"

"Yes," I said. "I've just arrived. I'm on my way to Winnipeg to meet my fiancé."

"Maybe you can answer my question. Tell me, why can't England fight her own battles? Every time they get into a war, they drag other countries in to finish what they start. My son was a brilliant boy, a good boy who had everything to live for. He died in a war that was none of his doing."

I was stunned. How could I respond to such a question? Finally, I looked at the woman. "I'm sorry you lost your son. The war is terrible. So many young people have died. It's a dreadful waste of lives and England certainly did not want a war. Many of our sons and daughters have died, too."

The woman did not respond.

I continued. "However, our country was threatened and if Britain falls, other countries will be invaded. Actually, your son was fighting for his country, too."

The woman picked up her toilet articles and left the restroom without looking at me.

I felt depressed when I went to the dining car for breakfast. I ordered toast and tea, and was deep in thought when I heard a voice ask, "May I join you?" I looked up to see a short, plump lady smiling at me.

"My name is Betty McGregor. I'm on my way to Winnipeg and since I'm traveling alone, I thought I'd find some company for breakfast."

I introduced myself and told the woman I'd be happy to have her company.

Over a second cup of tea, I told Betty about the lady in the restroom. "That's too bad you had that type of encounter with your first Winnipegger. They actually are very friendly people," she said.

When I told Betty I was going to marry Frank Dagg, the friendly lady replied, "What a coincidence. I know the Dagg family. They're a well-known family in Winnipeg. In fact, the father was one of the founders of the church I attend. Maude McCreery, the oldest sister, owns a large florist shop. She ran for councilwoman recently. She's a remarkable woman. You'll love her. Bob McCreery, her husband, owns a men's clothing store in the city. Frank is the youngest of eleven children. Four of the girls and two brothers live in Winnipeg."

I felt so much better. I enjoyed Betty's lively conversation. As I looked out the train window, the rugged Canadian terrain fascinated me—so different from the English pastoral scenery. I was amazed at the breathtaking mountains and the tall pine trees. I found it hard to imagine being on a train for two days and nights without falling off the end of the world. I knew I was about to live in a new and fascinating country.

Betty was wonderful company on the two-day journey. She told me about Winnipeg and warned me of the cold winters. "It gets way below zero, but we're all ready for it. In fact, fur coats aren't a luxury in our cold climate. Our houses are well-built and insulated. We have storm windows and good heating systems. In the winter we entertain a lot and of course, all our young people ice skate and ski. Our summers are hot and humid, so during those months we head for the lakes nearby."

As the train drew closer to Winnipeg, I wondered if Frank was as excited as I was. I wondered how he would look and how the family would accept me.

When the conductor passed through the compartments announcing we would arrive at Winnipeg in ten minutes, Betty gave me a card.

"Here's my name, address and telephone number. I do hope you'll call me when you're settled. I wish you all the luck in the world. You're going to be a member of a wonderful family."

I thanked Betty for being such good company and promised to keep in touch. Then I went to freshen up for the moment I'd been waiting for. I took one last look in the mirror before hurrying to the door where the porter was putting the steps down for us to leave the train. I trembled with excitement as I stepped onto the platform.

"Hello, Terrie," I heard someone say. I saw a tall slender man in a Canadian Mounted Police uniform. "I'm Don Anderson, Frank's brother-in-law. I'm married to Marguerite. Welcome to Winnipeg."

I hardly had time to respond when I heard two women arguing.

"I saw her first," said the shorter of the two.

"I recognized her right away." The other woman was taller and walked with a limp.

"Well, I was at the other exit, but I knew Terrie as soon as she got off the train."

"Okay, you two can argue that point later," Don said. "Terrie, this is Lydia and May, Frank's sister and sister-in-law. If you'll give me your claim check, I'll get your luggage."

Two men joined Lydia and May. One looked like an older version of Frank. The other stood a little shorter and was balding. Both men greeted me with a hug.

"I'm Pud," the one who looked like Frank said. "And this is Roy. The rest of the family is waiting at home. Maude and Bob could not get away from their businesses, and Marguerite and Dorothy are with their little boys. They're all anxious to meet you."

I was overwhelmed by all the confusion, especially when I remembered that Pud was Frank's brother, Albert. I finally found my voice. "Where's Frank? Is everything all right?"

Lydia took my arm. "You'll have to wait a few more days to see him. He was on leave in New York when the Queen Mary docked and he watched without knowing you were aboard. You see, your wire arrived after he left on a weekend leave and he didn't get it until he returned to the base. He's going to phone this afternoon so we have to hurry to Marguerite's house."

Don arrived with my luggage. "Let's get going," he said. "The girls will be getting anxious."

Roy told me I would be meeting his wife Annie and their two sons later.

"We'll see you back at the house," Pud said. "It's time for us to get back to work."

I felt terribly disappointed because Frank had not been at the station. However, my new family made me feel welcome as Don drove us to his home.

The store windows along the way fascinated me. I saw lots of colorful clothing in the department store windows and fruits and vegetables on display in the grocery stores. After Britain's austerity during the past few years, those sights were almost unreal to me.

Don pulled the car up in front of a large, two-story house where I could see two young women waiting on the porch. The taller one had a small boy holding her hand and the other held a baby. I hurried to meet them.

"Dorothy, I feel as if I know you already. Charlie has told me so much about you." I hugged the dark haired one with the small boy. "That's from Charlie. He sends his love to you both. He's fine and can hardly wait to be home with you and Tony."

The little boy looked happy. He had a smile like his daddy.

I turned to the young woman holding the baby. "Hi, Terrie," she said. "Welcome to the family. This is Derek. I kept him up from his nap to meet you."

Marguerite was attractive with a mass of brown curly hair. She hugged me with her free arm.

"I have to get back to the office," Don said. "I'll see you later. You girls can spend the afternoon chatting." Don kissed his wife and baby, and drove off.

"You are all so kind, I feel at home already. Don says Frank will be calling this afternoon."

Marguerite and Dorothy put Derek and Tony down for their naps and then Marguerite made tea. I felt comfortable with the women, Lydia and Pud's wife May. We became friends at once. As we were talking about my trip from Scotland, the phone rang. My heart skipped a beat. Marguerite called me to the phone. I heard Frank say, "Hi, there, honey."

All the anxieties of the last months seemed to vanish. "Oh, Frank, how wonderful to hear your voice." I was crying so hard I could hardly talk. "Your family is great. They've made me so welcome. When will I see you?"

"Well, let me see. This is Wednesday, the twelfth. Oh, by the way, how come you forgot that today is my birthday?"

"I'm not really sure what day this is. Happy birthday, sweetheart."

"Let's plan on being together for our birthdays from now on," Frank said.

"Mine's in a couple of weeks. We'll celebrate that one together."

"First, let's get married. How about Saturday? I can get a military plane out of here tomorrow morning. I'll go to Marguerite's right from the airport and be there by nine o'clock. I'm not permitted to say the exact time I'll arrive. I can hardly wait for a big hug from my girl. I love you so much."

After I hung up, I told everyone the news. "Well, if we're to have a wedding arranged by Saturday, we'd better get busy," Dorothy said.

"We'll have the reception here," Marguerite announced. "We don't have time to send out invitations, so we'll have to make up a list of guests and call them. I can do that." She turned to Dorothy. "I'll mind the boys while you take Terrie shopping for her wedding dress. She'll need other things, too. Thank goodness Maude will do the flowers and we can get Eaton's to do the catering."

Lydia spoke up. "You'll have to go to City Hall for your marriage license and also make arrangements to meet with Reverend Arnold at St. Philips Church. Our father was one of the founders of the church, so I'm sure you and Frank will want to have the ceremony there."

Dorothy suggested that I might consider having Jessie Dangerfield as my bridesmaid. "She's our sister May's granddaughter, a lovely girl about your age. You two look enough alike to be sisters."

As May said that, my thoughts went back to my family in England. I remembered the childhood plans Kathleen and I had made about being each other's bridesmaids. No one would be there to represent my family on the most important day of my life.

I quickly put those thoughts out of my mind and listened to Frank's three excited sisters chattering, making arrangements for my wedding.

"Well, we have a lot of family here. I don't think Chauncy and Ruth will be able to get here from Vancouver. However, our sister May will be coming to Winnipeg this week so hopefully she'll arrive by Saturday."

"Maude and Bob invited us for dinner tonight," Marguerite said. "We'd better get the boys up and dressed so we'll be ready when Don picks us up. Pud and May will meet us there. Terrie, you'll be staying with Maude and Bob until after the wedding."

Maude and Bob lived in a beautiful older home in

Winnipeg. Their two children, Jerry and Essie, had been born when their parents were in mid-life. Essie was fourteen and Jerry was sixteen. They were handsome youngsters, interested in hearing about England and the war. As soon as I met them, they bombarded me with questions.

Maude was a tall, attractive, large-boned woman. She wore her graying hair piled on top of her head in a French knot. Her eyes were ice blue and when she smiled, I couldn't help admiring her perfect teeth. Maude embraced me saying, "Welcome, dear. You're so young to have been through such a lot. I wrote to your family to let them know we'll love you and take care of you."

I gasped. What a thoughtful gesture.

"One day they'll realize they should be proud to have a daughter with your spirit and determination. However, I can understand how hard it must have been for them to let you go so far away, especially in wartime."

White-haired Bob Collins was the biggest man I'd ever seen. He was 6'6" and heavyset. As he took me in his arms, I almost lost my breath.

"Welcome, Terrie. I must say young Frank knows how to pick a wife. He's a swell guy and we're all proud of him. He's really done his share to help with this damn war."

At dinner, the whole family seemed to be talking at once about the wedding plans. Suddenly, I felt very tired. Lydia looked at me and said, "My dear, you must be exhausted. How could we be so thoughtless? We forgot what a long train journey you had, to say nothing of the emotional strain of the last few months. Come on girls, you can drop me off at home and let this poor child get to bed."

Dorothy told me she would be at Marguerite's early the next morning. "Maude will bring you to Marguerite's on her way to the store. It's too bad to have to rush you through the stores, but our time is limited. Frank said he'll be at Marguerite's in the morning. He couldn't tell us what time, so we'll have to wait for him."

After everyone left and Bob kissed me goodnight, Maude showed me to my room. The pretty flowered chintz drapes and bedspread matched the pale blue wallpaper and deeper blue carpet. The room felt restful.

"Have a good sleep, dear. I know your mind must be in turmoil. I understand how much you must miss your family. We're so happy to have you in ours."

I slept well that night much to my surprise, and awoke early to the touch of Maude's hand on my shoulder. "Time to get up. It's a beautiful day. We're lucky the snow is late this year."

The sun streamed through the window as I jumped out of bed to take a shower. "I'll be right down, Maude."

I dressed, brushed my hair and ran down to have breakfast with Maude and Bob. I couldn't believe the quantity of food that was available in Canada. That morning we had freshly squeezed orange juice. As I drank it, I thought of the children in England who had never seen an orange or a real egg. However, I was glad I'd lived in Britain during the war because I'd learned a lot about real values from my experiences. I knew family life, love and good health were all much more important than the material things in life.

As Frank's sisters were making the wedding arrangements, I remembered that it had been fourteen months since Frank had left

England. Would he have changed? Was I doing the right thing? So much had happened since we'd been together. And here I was in a different country with a new family.

Then the fears and doubts went away. I knew I loved Frank and that all would go well for us.

Maude dropped me at Marguerite's house a little after nine.

"Dorothy will be here at nine-thirty," Marguerite told me. Jessie is a legal secretary, but she's arranged to have a day off today. She'll be waiting for you and Dorothy at her apartment."

In the midst of all the chatter, I noticed a taxi stop in front of the house. I went to the door as Frank stepped out of the cab. My heart was pounding as I ran down the driveway to meet him. A moment later, I was in his arms. Tears ran down my cheeks as we held each other.

"I thought this day would never come," Frank said. "Let me look at you. You've grown taller since I left you in Nottingham."

I could hardly speak, my heart was so full. Finally, I said, "Everything's all right now that we're together. I was so lonely without you, Frank."

"Hey, you two," Marguerite called. "How about coming into the house before you both get colds?"

Under the sunny sky, the Winnipeg winds felt very cold. "Hey, Sis." Frank gave his sister a hug. "How are you and how's Don?"

Derek played happily in his playpen. Frank picked him up. "Hi, big fellow. You look just like a Dagg. Don't tell your dad I said that, though. I'm sure he wants you to look like him."

"We're going to be real busy for the next two days," I told Frank. "Your family's arranged for our wedding to be on Saturday at four. Marguerite is having the reception here. Today we get our marriage license and tomorrow we have to see the minister at St. Philips Church." I stopped to take a breath.

"Whoa there, Terrie. I might have known my family would jump into action right away. I thought we'd have a quiet wedding and be married by a J.P."

"Not a chance," Marguerite said. "Dorothy'll be here very soon to take Terrie shopping. They're picking up Jessie who'll be Terrie's bridesmaid. By the way, Mac Blair is in town. You'll probably want him to be your best man."

Frank and I stood with our arms around each other as Marguerite continued to tell Frank their plans. Then, Frank said, "I'll call Mac Blair at once. He and I have been friends since we were kids, Terrie. You'll like Mac. Unfortunately, he was unable to get into the service because he had TB when he was a child and his health is not too great."

"When you call him, tell him to meet you at St. Philips tomorrow. You and Terrie are to be there with Jessie and your best man to get your instructions for the ceremony."

"You guys have thought of everything. When do I get time with my bride?"

Dorothy and Tony arrived then. After greeting his sister, Frank lifted Tony high in the air and then they wrestled on the floor like two children, Tony loving every minute. Little Derek wanted to get out of his playpen. What a wonderful moment.

"Well, we have to get started. We'll see you later, Frank. We'll try to get everything done and meet you at three at Eatons. Then, you and Terrie can go to City Hall for your license. Maude says you can use her car today, so we'll take you to pick it up. You and Terrie are invited to have dinner with Pud and May tonight. Lydia'll be there, too."

They left Marguerite with the children and after dropping Frank at Maude's florist shop, Dorothy drove to Jessie's apartment. A plump, dark-brown-haired girl greeted us. She was about my age and we did sort of resemble each other.

"Isn't this exciting? I can hardly wait until Saturday," Jessie said.

Dorothy took us to a small dress shop. "Hello, Mrs. Jardine," the salesgirl said. "Is this the young lady from England? I have the very thing for her. I hope it'll be the right size."

We waited while the girl went into the back of the store. When she returned, she was carrying a wool suit in a lovely shade of periwinkle blue. I tried on the suit. It fit as if it had been tailored for me.

"Oh, I love the suit," I said as I stepped out of the dressing room, but may I speak to you privately, Dorothy?"

We went into the dressing room. "I'm embarrassed, Dorothy," I said. "You see, the ticket for my passage took almost all the money I had. I really cannot afford this suit."

"Oh, Terrie, how could I have been so foolish. I should have told you. Frank gave me the money for your dress and anything else you need. As soon as he knew you were coming, he sent money each week for you."

As the sales girl wrapped the suit for me, I couldn't remember when I'd been happier.

Jessie tried on a light tan wool dress. She looked very smart and decided to buy it. Our next stop was Eatons, the big department store. I bought black shoes and a black pillbox hat with tiny blue feathers.

Next, we went to the lingerie department and selected a pale blue negligee. I felt like a child at Christmas as I carried all the boxes.

"We have to get a coat for you. It'll be a gift from Maude. You're going to need a warm coat this winter."

We found a camel hair coat with a lynx collar that I loved. While they were getting it wrapped, I asked Dorothy if we could go to the book department.

"I know it sounds like a strange wedding gift, but I want to buy Frank a book on boat building. He wants to build our own sailboat one day. If I buy him a book about sailboats, he'll know I share his dream."

Dorothy agreed to take all the packages to Maude's. "That's where you'll be dressing for the wedding. Now it's time to meet Frank."

"Goodbye, I'll see you tomorrow," Jessie said. "Oh, I mean Saturday."

"Hi, girls. Did you get all your shopping finished?" Frank said.

I felt Frank's arms around me. I turned. "Thank you, Frank, for everything. I spent all your money, but we had a wonderful time picking out everything."

Dorothy interrupted. "Sorry to rush you, but you had better get to City Hall before they close. I have to hurry to Marguerite's to check on the boys. They can be a handful when they're together."

After we said goodbye to Dorothy and Jessie, Frank and I hurried to get our license.

"I do hope my family is not too much for you," Frank said. "They tend to try to manage things, but they mean well."

"I couldn't feel more comfortable," I told him. "They're all great."

As we applied for our license, I had to keep pinching myself to be sure I wasn't dreaming.

With our license tucked away in Frank's pocket, we went to the jewelry store and found a little gold locket for Jessie and a gold money clip for Mac.

"We'd better hurry so we won't be late for dinner," Frank said.

Frank drove us to a modest little house where May greeted us. The house was warm and filled with love. May and Pud had been married for fifteen years, had no children and were devoted to one another.

Lydia arrived a few minutes after we did. After giving each of us a hug, she said, "You have so much to do in such a short time. You must be exhausted, Terrie."

Pud told Frank how glad they were to have me join their family.

Pud was ten years Frank's senior. He and Roy had helped Lydia raise their younger brother after their parents had died.

The evening was lovely. May was a wonderful cook and prepared a beautiful dinner. After the English diet, everything tasted especially good. What a pleasant evening.

Frank took me back to Maude's.

"Goodnight, dear," Frank said. "I'm staying with Marguerite and Don. I'll be here in the morning and hopefully we can have a little time together before we have to meet Jessie and Mac at St. Philips."

As Frank left, I realized how much I wanted to be with him. I felt so much joy when we were together. I was lonely as I climbed into a strange bed, but a new chapter in my life was about to begin and that gave me the kind of excitement I knew I should be feeling upon the eve of my wedding.

After Frank left, I joined Maude and Bob in their living room before going to my room. "I want you both to know how grateful I am for everything you've done for me. Now, I have one more favor to ask. Bob, would you take my father's place at the wedding? I'd like you to walk me down the aisle."

"Of course, dear. I would consider it an honor."

When Frank arrived the next morning, we went for a long walk. Frank told me a little about his childhood in Winnipeg. Two rivers ran through the city, the Red River and the Assinoboine River. Wheat was their largest industry and hockey their most popular sport.

"We used to skate on the rivers when we were kids. Winnipeg is a great place for raising a family. However, I don't plan to live here once I get out of the service. I want to live near the ocean so we can sail that boat we'll be building."

"I don't mind where we live as long as we're together," I said. "If we move away, I'll miss your family. But, I'll go wherever you feel is right for us."

Soon the time arrived for us to meet our attendants, Mac and Jessie. The two of them were already at the church talking with a middle-aged man wearing a clerical collar.

"Well, if it isn't little Frankie Dagg," the minister teased. "I guess it takes a pretty English girl to get you into my church. I haven't seen you here for some time."

"Well, I may not have been able to get to church since I've been overseas. Believe me, I've felt very close to God on many occasions the past few years."

Frank introduced me to Reverend Arnold and also to his old friend, Mac Blair, a tall, slender young man with a shy smile and quiet manner.

"Did you know that Frank's father was one of the founders of this church?" Reverend Arnold said. "The Daggs are a fine family. They come from sturdy Irish-Swedish stock. You'll love them all."

After Reverend Arnold instructed the four of us regarding our parts in the wedding ceremony, he asked Frank and me to join him in his study.

We sat down and listened intently while the minister talked with us about the seriousness of the marriage contract.

"As the years pass, you'll have many challenges. Sometimes it will seem easier to give up, but you must remember the vows you'll take tomorrow. You'll never regret the sacrifices you may make in order to be a good husband, wife and parent. The secret is to always be able to communicate with each other, always talk your troubles out, be honest with one another and never go to sleep at night until everything is right between you. Run along now and I'll see you tomorrow. You have my very best wishes for a long and happy life together."

I was so glad we'd be married in a church rather than by a Justice of the Peace. I didn't have much to say as we drove back to Maude's house.

"A penny for your thoughts," Frank said.

"I guess I'm a little homesick. I keep wishing my family could be here tomorrow. I've hurt my parents, Frank. After all that's happened, we have to make sure our marriage is a happy one."

"Honey, you're just getting last minute nerves. I love you and have no doubt we'll have a wonderful and meaningful life together. When we give your parents their first grandchild, all will be forgiven. Just wait, you'll see," Frank told me.

Bob was waiting to meet us. "As usual, I have instructions for you." He laughed. "Terrie is to be at Marguerite's by six-thirty and Frank, you're to come back here. We'd better do as we're told."

After a quick shower, I changed my clothes. Frank took me to Marguerite's where Lydia greeted us at the door. We walked into the living room and my eyes grew bigger as I heard, "Surprise!" from every corner of the room. All Frank's sisters and sisters-in-law were there along with Jessie, Mac's wife Phyllis, and some other women friends of the family. After I recovered from the shock, Dorothy introduced me to everyone.

"Now I know why you said you'd see me tonight, Jessie," I said. "This is a wonderful surprise."

"The boys are giving Frank a stag party at Bob's. You won't be seeing him until the wedding.

I received some handsome luggage, lovely lingerie and household gifts. I was overwhelmed by the warmth of those people I hardly knew. My friend Betty McGregor was right, Winnipeggers were friendly and hospitable.

The party broke up quite late and Maude drove me home. The house was quiet as we checked the rooms. "I guess the boys are out on the town. Let's just go to bed. You must be tired and I know I am," Maude said. "Besides, you have an early appointment at the beauty parlor in the morning."

I dreamt about my family in England that night. Kathleen and I were children again and planning what our weddings would be like when we grew up. I dreamed about Edith and wished my old friend could be with me. In my dream, I was a child and my parents watched me perform at my dance recital. They were so proud of me.

When I awoke the next morning, it took me several moments to realize where I was. I soon remembered as my room filled with sunshine. Maude and Bob were eating breakfast when I joined them in the dining room.

"Your appointment is in an hour, dear, so you have time for

breakfast. Did you sleep well?" Maude said.

I managed to eat some toast with my tea and soon Maude and I were on our way to the beauty parlor. I had a facial, manicure and my hair shampooed and arranged. I felt pampered and relaxed, a new experience for me.

"You look lovely," Maude said. "Let's go home so you can rest for an hour before we have to get ready to leave for the church."

After a brief nap, I dressed in my new blue suit and hat, then walked downstairs where Maude and Bob were waiting. I began to tremble when I realized I would be Mrs. Frank Dagg in a few hours. And my life would have a new beginning.

Maude said, "We know you miss your family, but they'll come around when you send them pictures of the wedding."

"Thank you, Maude. I hope you're right. The British are stubborn people. I wish things could have been different." I missed my family with all my heart.

Maude left for the church and a few minutes later, Bob helped me into his car. "Well, dear, this is a first for me, too. I guess we'll hold each other up."

Bob and I waited in the anteroom with Jessie. Maude had filled the church with flowers from The Rosary. She had bouquets for Jessie and me. I carried white baby roses with lily of the valley and baby's breath. Jessie's bouquet was yellow baby roses and a delicate fern.

Jessie gave me a quick glance before she started her walk down the red-carpeted aisle when the wedding march began. Then, I felt Bob give my arm a squeeze as he said, "Come on, Terrie. It's time for our walk."

I could see Frank waiting at the altar with Mac. Frank wore his RCAF uniform and had a proud smile on his face. Mac, who appeared to be more nervous than Frank, looked very smart in his dark suit. As I reached the altar, Bob gave Frank my hand and I heard Frank whisper, "You're beautiful. I love you."

After we said our vows, we kissed for the first time as husband and wife. Then we turned and walked up the aisle facing the smiling faces of Frank's family and friends, and now mine. A small voice inside me said, "Please forgive me, Mom and Dad. Be happy for us."

Dozens of people attended a wonderful reception at Marguerite's. Frank saw friends he'd gone to school with, and even some of his grade-school teachers. Amazing how our wedding and reception had been arranged in just three days. The hors d'oeuvres were wonderful. Champagne flowed and everyone was in happy spirits. The photographer took lots of pictures and made many toasts. Don and Bob each made toasts. Our wedding was truly an unforgettable day.

Finally, Frank took me aside and said, "I think it's time for us to leave. Maude and Bob have reserved a room for us at the Fort Garry. It's the finest hotel in Winnipeg. We have to leave on the afternoon train for Montreal. Annie, Roy's wife, is having a family breakfast tomorrow morning before we leave."

Jessie caught my bouquet, but before I threw it over my shoulder, I took one of the tiny roses out to press in my prayer book. After Frank and I cut the first piece, Dorothy cut the three-tiered wedding cake for our guests. Dorothy promised to keep the top tier in her freezer so Frank and I could have it to celebrate on our first anniversary.

Frank and I ran to Maude's car amidst a shower of rice and good wishes, then we drove to the beautiful old Fort Garry Hotel overlooking the Assinoborne River. We found a bottle of champagne and a gorgeous flower arrangement in our spacious room. Frank's family had remembered everything.

When we settled in our room, Frank gave me a little package. Its wrapping was so pretty, I didn't want to open it. Inside was an exquisite evening purse — black peau de soie with pettipoint embroidered on the flap. Inside I found a penny. "That's for good luck, dear. I'll always love you. May today be the beginning of a wonderful life together."

Frank poured a glass of champagne for each of us, after which I handed Frank the gift I'd bought for him. "It's not the usual kind of gift, but it has lots of meaning."

When Frank opened the package, he was ecstatic. "Honey, with both of us sharing the same dreams, we can't go wrong. I'm the luckiest guy in the world."

As Frank took me in his arms, I think he sensed my apprehension. Neither my mother nor Edith had ever discussed that part of married life with me. I so wanted to please Frank. My worry was for nothing. Frank was very patient and gentle in his lovemaking. I can't describe the joy I felt. As we were falling asleep in each other's arms, I said, "I'm so glad we waited, Frank. Let's pray we'll always be as happy as we are tonight."

"Good morning, Mrs. Dagg," Frank said as I awoke. The bedside clock said ten. I snuggled close to Frank. "I wish we could stay here all day."

"So do I." He sighed.

"But I guess we have to get to Roy's for breakfast."

The whole family was at Roy's. I couldn't believe the amount of food. The Dagg's were hardy people with healthy appetites. Everyone talked at once as we all enjoyed the breakfast. Frank and I opened our wedding gifts, which Maude offered to store for us until we had a place of our own.

We received lovely pieces of silver, porcelain, bone china, a blanket from the famous Hudson's Bay Company, and small appliances.

"I'll be very busy writing thank you notes. I'd better get all the addresses before we leave," I said.

Soon, it was time for us to go to the station. I wore the coat Maude and Bob gave me. Everyone hugged and kissed us. They told us to write as soon as possible with our address. I felt a moment of sadness. It seemed as if I was leaving another family, but then I remembered I was not alone this time.

When we found our compartment on the train, we were surprised to see a big basket of fruit waiting for us. "Your family is so generous, Frank. I wish we could have stayed in Winnipeg. I love them all already. I'll really miss them when we're in Montreal."

"We'll be back, but remember, there's still a war to be won. I have no idea what my orders will be when I get back to the base."

Frank arranged to rent a room for us in a nice house not far from his base in Montreal. The French Canadians who owned the house spoke fluent English. Our room was small but clean. We shared a bathroom with another couple. I felt terribly lonely when Frank left to go to the base. My life had changed so much in such a short time. I was in a strange place with nothing to keep me busy except writing thank you letters. I finally realized I'd not been alone since I'd arrived in Winnipeg. One afternoon I decided to venture out to explore Montreal. I caught a bus, but the driver apparently didn't speak English or he just decided not too. After trying to communicate with him and a couple of other people when I asked for directions, I decided Montreal wasn't as friendly as Winnipeg. When Frank arrived home from work, he had a serious expression on his face.

"Well, honey. I guess you're going to have to go back to Winnipeg. I got my orders and I'm to be sent to the Pacific to help fight the Japs. After I take my physical exam, I'll be leaving."

"Oh, Frank, how can I stand losing you again? When will this war ever be over?"

In a few days, we had made arrangements for my return to Winnipeg. "I guess you'll have your first Canadian Christmas without me, honey. Things are not exactly working out as we hoped. But, the family will take care of you."

We wrote to Marguerite and Don to ask if I could stay with them until I could find an apartment. I could help her with Derek and it would give me something to keep myself busy. My heart was heavy as I wondered if Frank and I would ever be together again.

I was very disappointed as I heard nothing from my family, but I did get letters from Edith telling me everyone was well. Mamie also wrote telling me all the news from the Y. Everyone was fine and promised to keep in touch.

I missed Frank terribly when I moved back to Winnipeg. One morning, about two weeks after I was settled at Marguerite's, Don answered the phone. "Terrie, it's Frank. He says he has good news."

I picked up the phone to hear Frank say, "Hi, honey. I hope you're sitting down. I have some good news. I'll be home before you know it."

"Why, Frank, what happened? Is anything wrong? Did they end the war and not tell us?"

"It's not quite that good, but I guess the war is over for me. When I took my physical, they discovered a problem with my right ear. The engine noise and gunfire apparently did some

damage when I was flying as a gunner. It's not serious, but I'll
not be eligible to fly. I'll be stationed near Winnipeg, probably as
ground crew."

"How wonderful, but you must be terribly disappointed.
You worked so hard to earn your wings."

"Well, I admit it was a shock. It seems like such a little thing
to wipe me out of flying. I'll have to concentrate on sailing, now.
Maybe after the war, I can do some commercial flying. The good
thing is, we can be together very soon and start planning our
future."

Again, emotions ranged from happy to sad. I was elated
that at last we'd be together on a more permanent basis. I was
sad that Frank had lost some hearing in his right ear, but I realized
things could be a lot more serious considering what could have
happened during the flights he made over Germany and Italy
from 1939 to 1941.

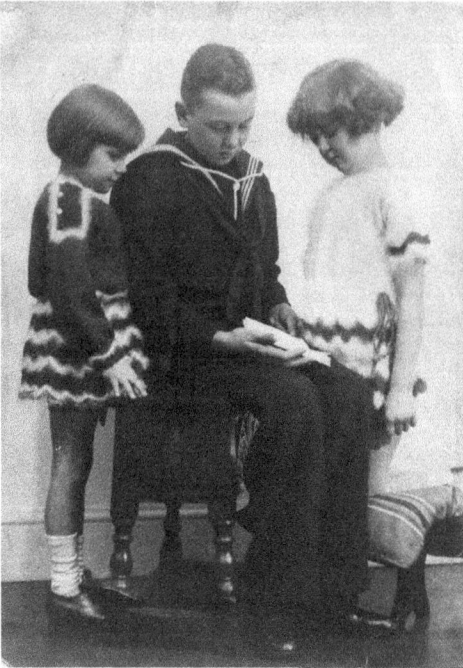

Above: Billy, Kathleen and me in 1937. Nursemaid Edith knitted our dressses.

Top right: At a seaside resort at Skegness, England. I always adored my big brother.

Bottom: Dad, Mom and me at age 8, with my nursemaid Edith. We were in the garden at the back of our house in Nottingham.

*We were interviewed outside Buckingham Palace after the
Investiture 1943. I was so proud of Frank.*

BUCKINGHAM PALACE.

2848

Admit one to witness the Investiture.

30 MAR 1943

Clarendon

Lord Chamberlain.

MISS T. ALLEN

VISIT TO PALACE

Nottm. Girl Went To Investiture

AMONG those attending an investiture at Buckingham Palace recently was a Nottingham girl who accompanied a Canadian flight-sergeant.

Miss Terrie Allen, who is the youngest daughter of Mr. and Mrs. F. L. Allen, of 32, Ramsdale-crescent, Mapperley, met Flight-sergeant Francis (Frank) G. Dagg, of Winnipeg, in connection with her work as assistant manageress of the Y.M.C.A. Canteen, Nottingham.

Flight-sergeant Dagg, who is 29, was awarded the D.F.M. The citation reads: "He has been in the most heavily defended areas in Germany. He has never missed an opportunity of attacking gun posts and searchlights, and on several occasions in combat with enemy fighters his unfailing alertness and accurate shooting have undoubtedly prevented serious attacks from developing. He is an air-gunner of outstanding ability."

Flight-sergt. Dagg has been in this country for about 2½ years and has made 35 trips over enemy territory, including participation in the 1,000-bomber raid on Cologne and recent raid on Genoa.

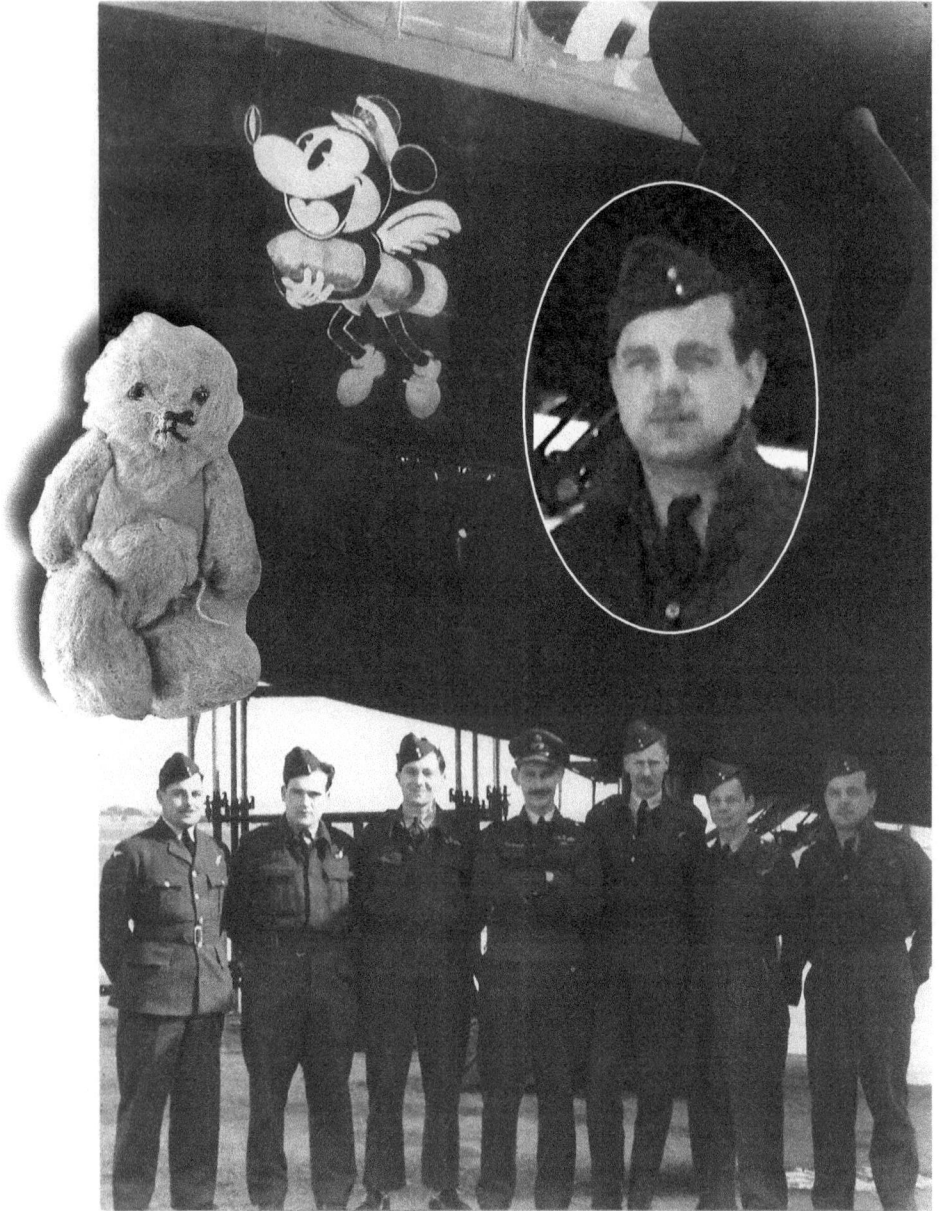

Frank was the mid-upper-turret gunner on the Lancaster Bomber. I had given Frank the teddy bear for good luck.

Wing Commander John Wooldrich, DFC (center) led Squadron 106 of the RCAF on many successful bombing missions.

CANADA

MINISTER OF NATIONAL DEFENCE FOR AIR

Miss Lydia Dagg,
44 Cromwell Street,   OTTAWA
Norwood Grove,   March 22nd, 1943.
MANITOBA.

Dear Miss Dagg:

I am writing to say how much all ranks of the Royal
Canadian Air Force join with me in warmly congratulating you and the
members of your family on the honour and distinction which have come
to your brother Flight Sergeant Francis George Dagg DFM, through the
award of the Distinguished Flying Medal for great gallantry in the
performance of his duty while serving with No. 106 Squadron of the
Royal Air Force.

The citation on which this award was made reads as
follows:

"Flight Sergeant Dagg has taken part in operational
sorties on the most heavily defended areas in Germany. He has never missed the opportunity of attacking
gun posts and searchlights and on several occasions,
in combats with enemy fighters, his unfailing alertness and accurate shooting have prevented serious
attacks developing. He is an air gunner of outstanding
ability and by his devotion to duty, both in the air
and on the ground, has set a high example to all."

The personnel of the Force are proud of your brother's
fine Service record.

Yours sincerely,

"Minister of National Defence for Air"

Frank's sister Lydia received this letter. She asked me to keep it for Frank.

Reverend Arnold watched as we signed the register after the ceremony.

The reception. The Dagg family and friends. A truly memorable day, just three days after I arrived in Winnipeg.

DAY TO DAY

Nottingham Y.M.C.A. Romance: Wedding Bells in Canada

AN engagement which had its beginnings over the coffee cups at a Nottingham canteen is shortly to culminate in a wedding in Canada.

The bride-to-be is Miss Terrie Allen, for the past two-and-a-half years assistant manageress at the Y.M.C.A. canteen, Shakespeare-street, and her fiance is Warrant Officer F. G. Dagg, D.F.M., of the Royal Canadian Air Force, who until a year or so ago was stationed in the Nottingham district, and was a frequent visitor to the canteen. When he was awarded the D.F.M Miss Allen accompanied him to Buckingham Palace for the investiture.

Farewell Gifts

AFTER completing his tour of operations, Warrant Officer Dagg was recalled to Canada, where he is now an instructor, Miss Allen is shortly sailing to join him, and will stay with his family in Winnipeg until the wedding.

Among her wedding gifts are a series of presentations from the Y.M.C.A., where she has been a most popular member of the staff. The local council of the association, the staff at

English Girl Weds in Winnipeg

A young bride who arrived this week from Great Britain plighted her troth Saturday, at 4.30 p.m., at St. Philip's church, Norwood when Frances Teresa, daughter of Mr. and Mrs. Frank Leslie Allen 32 Ramsdale crescent, Sherwood Nottingham, England, became the bride of WO.2 Frank G. Dagg R.C.A.F. Rev. G. Gillespie officiated. Mrs. D. McKidd presided at the organ, playing the wedding music.

The bride, given in marriage by J. R. McCreery, wore a dressmaker suit of azure blue wool, made on simple lines. Her small hat was veiled and trimmed with matching blue breast feathers. She wore Victoria roses.

Miss Jessie Dangerfield attended the bride and McCrea Blair, Jr., was groomsman. The ushers were two nephews of the bridegroom, Roy and Merrill Dagg.

A reception was held at the home of the bridegroom's sister, Mrs. D. K. Anderson, 946 Jessie avenue. Later the couple left for Three Rivers, Que., where they will make their home. For travelling Mrs. Dagg donned a topcoat of camel hair wool with collar and trim of natural lynx. She wore orchids.

OCTOBER. 14th '944

Frank and I were finally together. It had been a long separation.

WO. Frank Dagg Back In Winnipeg

Warrant Officer Frank Dagg, a Winnipeg airmen who completed 35 bombing raids as an air gunner overseas and won the D.F.M., returned to the city over Trans-Canada Airlines, Thursday. He explained he will be married here, Saturday, to Miss Terry Allen, Nottingham, England, who arrived with the party of English girls, Wednesday.

Warrant Officer Dagg recently completed a pilot's course in eastern Canada.

He and his financee are guests of his sister, Mrs. J. R. McCreery, 177 Oak street.

OCT: 12th. 1944.

Chapter 6

The war ended a few months after Frank returned to
Winnipeg. Frank was awarded an honorable discharge with a
small pension for his ear problem.

He never spoke much about his bomber raids over Germany
and Italy. He had great respect for Wing Commander John
Wooldridge, and for the well-known Wing Commander Guy
Gibson who led the famous 1000 bomber raid over Cologne.

I remember Frank telling me that he would probably never
drink orange juice again. The airmen were given orange juice
for energy before each mission. They had probably killed many
women and children on the raids. Orange juice was a reminder.

He also mentioned that the raids over Germany had much
more activity from searchlights and anti-aircraft fire than the ones
over Italy.

Frank and I stayed with Marguerite and Don for a short while until we found a tiny one-room apartment in an old building in downtown Winnipeg. "It's not palatial, but it'll be our own little home," I told Frank. "We'll get it all fixed up and make it cozy and then we can have the family over for dinner. They've all been so good to us."

I had fun making blue chintz draperies and a matching cover for the day-bed that doubled as our bed. We went to a second-hand store and found a dining table and two chairs, two end tables and a chest of drawers. Maude gave us a rug for a wedding gift and we bought two lamps. We received a set of bright colored towels as wedding gifts that brightened up our tiny bathroom.

In the kitchen, we had an old stove and icebox against one wall, but we had to use the washbasin in the bathroom for washing our dishes. Frank built a wooden cover to put over the stove when it was not in use. Soon, our kitchen-dining room looked warm and lived-in.

Marguerite, Don, Dorothy and Charlie gave us a picture of a ballerina as a wedding gift. The white frame with an intricate design looked perfect over the couch in our living room-bedroom. They knew of my ballet background. The picture was a beautiful and thoughtful gift.

As we worked to fix up our one-room apartment, we spent many happy hours together. When we were out, we had to watch the clock to be sure to get home before the water ran over from the melting ice in our ice box.

Even though Frank enrolled in a woodworking class, he wasn't happy. He found it difficult to get back into civilian life after the excitement he had experienced during his war years.

I heard regularly from Edith. She wrote that everyone in

the family was fine and that Marjorie had kept her promise and was visiting her often. Even though I wrote Mom and Dad many times, I never received a reply.

One day, Frank came home and asked, "How'd you like to go to California."

"California?"

"Yes. It's not really an impulsive idea. I've been thinking about it for some time."

"You have? I didn't know that."

"Terrie, I know I can never fly commercial planes with my ear problem, but I'm sure I can get a job as a carpenter with one of the movie studios in Hollywood."

"This is very sudden, Frank."

"I know, I know, but honey, wouldn't it be great? We could start building our sailboat."

"Won't we have to apply for visas to move to the states?" I said. "This all sounds a little scary, Frank."

"We'll go to the Immigration Department. They'll tell us what the procedure is."

Frank was always confident things would be okay.

The next day, the immigration officer told us we'd need to have a sponsor, someone who lived in the states, since we didn't have the necessary amount of money required for a permanent visa. Frank wrote Hilda James, a distant cousin who lived in Hollywood. She wrote back saying she would be willing to sponsor us. We were so grateful.

"See, Terrie. Sounds like things are meant to be," Frank said. "I'm sure Hilda will steer us in the right direction once we tell her our plans."

I tried to be optimistic about another move. My confidence

in Frank didn't falter. However, I was going to be in a different
country again where we'd have to find a new home, get jobs
and make new friends. The thought was a little frightening, yet
intoxicating. Being married to Frank was not going to be dull.

"You're taking a big chance, Frank," cautioned Pud.
"There're a lot of American servicemen who're back home looking
for jobs. At least, if you're going to do it, you're young enough to
give it a try."

Once again, I packed our belongings. Maude agreed to store
them until Frank and I found a place to live in the states. Frank
sold the few pieces of furniture we owned. I was sad when we left
our tiny apartment, our home of just a few months.

Everyone in the family came to the bus depot to see us off.
They wished us well as we boarded the Greyhound Bus for the
five-day trip to California.

Dorothy hugged me. "Charlie will be home any day now,"
she said. "He'll be disappointed to find you're in California. He
was so anxious to see you and Frank."

Our trip by bus was long and tiring. We managed to get two
vacant seats along the back of the bus so we could stretch out and
try to sleep. I was still amazed at our plans.

I found it fascinating to watch the scenery change as the bus
made its way through Minnesota, Montana, Idaho and on down
the Pacific Coast. The further south the bus went the greener and
more picturesque the scenery became. Oregon was beautiful. We
both wished we could spend more time there, but the bus stops
were short.

The United States was big, and everything seemed to move
fast. I noticed, though, that each state had its own differences.
The rugged countryside of Winnipeg was very different from the

forests we rode through along the magnificent West Coast.

I was thrilled when I first caught sight of the Pacific Ocean. It looked more blue and calm than the Atlantic. Somehow, I imagined the Pacific to be warmer. I wanted to jump right in and play in the surf. I told Frank how excited I felt to see the beautiful countryside as we traveled south toward California.

When we arrived in Los Angeles, we found a city bus that would take us to Hollywood. Los Angeles traffic was confusing, so busy and crowded. I could hardly believe we were really in Hollywood as we walked the city streets. "When I was growing up," I told Frank, "I dreamt about Hollywood. Who would ever have thought that one day I would actually be here?"

"Once we're settled, we can start exploring. I'm sure we'll love it here."

We walked from the bus stop to an apartment building a few blocks away and found the address of our sponsor. We rang the doorbell. We were greeted by a short, middle-aged woman with a stern look on her face.

"Hello, Hilda," Frank said. "This is my wife, Terrie. Do you remember when my parents brought me here as a child?"

"Well, I don't remember, but I agreed to sponsor you, so I'm glad you made it here. I'm not inviting you in because you can't stay here. I live alone and don't have the room. You'll have to get a place of your own."

"We want to thank you for sponsoring us, but we have no intention of imposing on you, Hilda," Frank said. "We just need your help to give us an idea where to look for a place to live. . .a few directions so we can find our way around."

"I know a couple who rents rooms. I'll give you directions to their house. I'll call to let them know you're on your way."

Frank and I were completely shocked, hurt and unable to believe that she would treat us that way. I was crying because I'd thought we'd be meeting a friend. I hoped everyone in Hollywood wouldn't be so unfriendly.

Frank said, "You don't need to cry, Terrie. We'll find a place. At least we know where we stand with Hilda. We'll make it on our own, honey."

When we knocked on the door of the house Hilda sent us to, a plump lady with a friendly smile greeted us. I liked Mrs. Silverman at once. Her husband, a small man, came into the hallway. He shook Frank's hand as he welcomed us.

"The room I have is small, but it has a pretty view of the ocean. You'll have to share the bathroom. I can allow you to make light meals in the kitchen, but you'll have to eat dinners out."

She showed us a bright, clean room on the second floor.

"Is this okay?" Frank said.

I felt more encouraged knowing we had a place to live. I knew things were going to be fine. "It's perfect, Frank." I once again felt excited. "Let's pay for our room and then we can start looking for jobs. Before you know it, everything will fit into place."

After a shower and a change of clothes, both of us felt better. We headed for the bus stop. Frank took the bus that went to the movie studios. I headed downtown. I decided to try for a job in one of the department stores. Neither of us was successful that first day. We bought a paper and circled places to try the next day.

That night, we wrote to the family in Winnipeg to tell them that everything was going well. I wrote an airmail letter to my mom and dad so they'd know our new address.

As the days passed by, we'd meet each other at dinner time and discuss our job-hunting. Frank got discouraged. He'd learned that unless he was a union member, the studios couldn't hire him. The carpenters union was a closed shop. Things didn't look too promising unless he could find some other type of work.

We decided we needed transportation in order to look for work. Checking the ads, Frank found a used black Ford for a reasonable price. The clunker served its purpose.

On the fourth day of job hunting, I got a job in the sportswear department of Myer-Seigle, a large clothing store. I could hardly wait to tell Frank the good news.

"I'm so happy for you, dear, but I'm sorry that you'll be the breadwinner. I don't seem to be having any luck at all and our money is getting tight."

"You'll get something, soon," I said. "Now that I have a job, there has to be one for you. Our luck is getting better. We'll be okay."

I enjoyed my job. I liked the girls I worked with. My English accent seemed to delight the customers. I was tired after being on my feet all day, but happy to be earning money.

Two weeks later, I arrived at the house to find Frank waiting with a look of defeat on his usually happy face. "Terrie, we may have to give up. If I don't land something soon, our money will be gone. I have to keep enough for the trip home and your salary just covers the rent."

"Oh, Frank, you'll find work."

"I feel like I've failed you, Terrie. Tomorrow will be our first anniversary and I've not been a good provider."

My heart went out to my husband. I felt so bad to see his disappointment. I put my arms around him. "You provide me with love. You're kind and considerate. That's the important thing. Every young couple has a hard time at first. That's why they always say the first year is the hardest."

The following day, we made a decision. If Frank didn't get a job by the week-end, we'd go back to Winnipeg.

When there was a tap on our door that evening, Frank answered to find Mrs. Silverman outside, holding a yellow envelope in her hand.

My heart felt like it was in my throat as I saw what must be a telegram. I knew it had to be from England.

"This cable just arrived. I hope it's not bad news," Mrs. Silverman said.

I took the telegram. I knew it would be good news. "Oh, Frank, Mom and Dad remembered our first anniversary. This telegram must be their way of telling us everything is okay, now."

I tore open the envelope. As I read the message, my heart sank. I was lightheaded. I didn't want to believe the words I read.

"What is it, dear?" Frank said. He took the cable and read, "Mother died in her sleep on October 13. Regrets, Dad."

As Frank held me in his arms, I cried as if my heart would break. "Now I'll never be able to make things right. Mother never forgave me. How will I ever make her know how happy we are together? Did I break her heart? Is this my fault?"

I thought my tears would never stop. I would have to live the rest of my life without ever telling my mother I was sorry I had to leave her."

Frank tried to console me. I'm sure he knew it would take a long time for me to get over the shock and disappointment.

"Terrie," Frank finally said. "I'm going to put a call through to your father. You should have some contact with your family at this time."

"That would be wonderful, Frank. I feel so far away from them, but it costs too much to telephone them in England. We're very short of money and we have to get back to Winnipeg."

"We have to do what is right. We'll manage."

We went downstairs to use the phone in the hall. We waited and waited until finally, the operator said, "Go ahead."

"Oh, Daddy, I'm so sorry. I love you and I loved Mommy so much." There was so much static on the line I could hardly hear my father's voice.

"It's all right, dear," I heard my father say. "She loved you, too. She just didn't want to give you up. I realize now that we were wrong to try to run your life."

I couldn't keep from crying.

"Mother died very peacefully in her sleep. The funeral was beautiful. Many friends attended and the flowers were gorgeous. You remember your mother always loved flowers. You and Frank take care of each other. Maybe you'll be able to come home for a visit one of these days."

After Dad and I hung up, Frank and I knelt by the bed and said a silent prayer for my mother. We both knew that every wedding anniversary from then on would be a reminder of my mother's death. She had died one day before.

Two days later, Frank and I swallowed our pride and took the bus back to Winnipeg.

"I'm determined to try again." Frank said. "Next time we'll make it. And one day we'll build that boat and sail it on San Francisco Bay.

Everyone in the family was happy to see us when we returned to Winnipeg. We were grateful that nobody made us feel as if we'd failed. The family was very sad to know that my mother had passed away. Marguerite and Don invited us to stay with them until we could find a place to live and Frank could find work.

"Terrie, you were a big help with Derek and the house when you were here before. I really missed you. We're happy to have you back," Marguerite said.

When we visited Dorothy and Charlie, Frank thanked him for the support he had given me when he was in England.

In a few days, Frank found a job working in the office of a cement company. Although we were happy with Marguerite and Don, we really wanted a home of our own, so we started looking for a place to live.

One day, Frank called me during his lunch time. "Guess what?" he said, excited. "A fellow at work just told me that some homes are being built in Charleswood for veterans. There're only building a few and selling them on a first-come, first-serve basis. My boss has given me the afternoon off. Get your coat and I'll pick you up in fifteen minutes." We still didn't have a car, but public transportation was good.

When we arrived at the Veteran's Administration office, four home sites were still available. Frank qualified. We signed the application papers and were directed to where the homes were being built.

Charleswood was on the outskirts of the city, about a half mile from the nearest bus stop. Many of the homes were already constructed. We were shown a model of the one we'd be able to buy.

"How do you feel about living out here?" Frank said. "It'll be a good start. I'm sorry it's such a long way out of town, but you'll make friends quickly."

"It's a dream," I said. "The only thing that worries me is the walk you'll have to and from the bus stop each day. You'll have to leave real early and you'll be home late. It'll be tough in the winter."

A few weeks later, we moved into the little house on Pepperloaf Crescent. We bought a few pieces of furniture, unpacked the boxes we'd had in storage, and soon we'd made the house into a warm home. I spent long days digging up the hard ground and trying to plant flowers and vegetables. Most of our neighbors were couples about my age. I made a lot of friends.

In December, 1946, I suspected I was pregnant. I decided to see a doctor. I didn't want to tell Frank until I was sure my suspicions were correct. Dorothy recommended a physician so I made an appointment for the following week.

"My father delivered some of the Dagg babies," Dr. Benoit told me. "He retired a few years ago and I took over his practice." After he examined me, Dr. Benoit said, "Well, young lady, you should deliver a son or daughter late in July. You're fine. I'll see you next month."

I made a special dinner that night and even bought a bottle of wine for a toast.

"What's the occasion? Did I forget something?" Frank said.

"How would you feel about becoming a father?" I waited for Frank's response.

Frank gave me a big hug. "When? Why didn't you tell me before? You must take it easy, now. No more gardening for you. We must think of a name for her."

"Whoa," I said as I snuggled in Frank's arms. "First, I'm fine and exercise is good for me. Dr. Benoit says the baby should be born in late July. Why're you so sure we'll have a daughter? I think we'd better think of a few boys' names, too."

The family was delighted when I told them the news. I wrote to Edith and my father at once.

The next few months went by fast. I loved to knit and spent many hours making booties and little jackets, mostly in white. I wrote down boys and girls names as I thought of those that would work with Dagg. Our surname wasn't an easy one to put a name with.

We spent a very cold, harsh winter in Charleswood. Many days were below zero. Walking to the bus stop was a hazard. Frank would break the snow each morning, and arrive home at night quite late. The days were long for both of us.

The snow was deep even after it was plowed. We stayed in the house and enjoyed reading. Sometimes we'd get together with our new friends and play card games in the evenings or listen to the radio.

One Saturday, when I was in my sixth month, May and Pud invited us to have dinner with them. We took a bus and decided to get off about a mile from Pud's house to walk and enjoy the spring day.

A lot of homes were being built in the area. I noticed one on a corner that reminded me of a doll house. The small house had white stucco exterior walls with red trim around the windows. A black wrought-iron railing had been built on either side of the steps that led to the front door.

"Let's peek in the windows," I said. "It's such a cute little house."

We started with the big window in the front. The large kitchen was painted white with red linoleum and knotty pine cabinets. As we walked around to look in the other windows, we saw there were two bedrooms and a large living room. The floors were beautiful hardwood. The builder had a sign in one of the windows.

"Let's take the number and call the builder from Pud's," Frank said. "It's really a nice place. I'd like to know the price and maybe take a look inside."

We were excited as we walked on to Pud's. Before we took off our coats, we called the builder and found him at home.

"I'm asking six thousand dollars for that house. If you'd like to see inside, I can meet you there with a key."

May and Pud went with us to meet the builder. We were all impressed with the construction and layout of the house.

Pud said, "It's a lot of money, Frank, but if you think you can swing it, now's the time to do it. It's a perfect place for a small family and we'd love to have you living close to us."

I knew we'd buy the house on Braemar Avenue as we walked through the rooms. I felt sure we were meant to live there. We had just enough money for the down payment from the sale of our house in Charleswood.

Though the two bedrooms, one bath were quite small, we decided it would be perfect when our baby came. The house did have a big kitchen with a nice eating area, plus a large living room and basement.

We were close to a bus stop and much closer to family. And we had wonderful neighbors. Life was good.

Then, we had a setback. The company Frank worked for went bankrupt and Frank was laid off. He came home one day to tell me he was job hunting again.

"Don't worry, honey," he said. "I'll find something soon. There are other jobs in Winnipeg."

Pud called to tell Frank he heard of a job with the Canadian National Railway. Frank applied and was accepted. He became a block operator working on the night shift. I didn't like being alone at night, but I knew I had to get used to it. At least we enjoyed having afternoons and evenings together.

Nearer to the time our baby was to be born, Maude gave us a crib and highchair that had been used for her children. Dorothy and Marguerite had a baby shower for me. I received lovely gifts from the family and friends. Our baby would be well-dressed.

Life had never seemed so stable. I felt we were finally establishing a lifestyle.

The summer in Winnipeg was hot and humid. I was uncomfortable in July as my delivery date drew closer.

One Wednesday morning, I was baking cookies when I felt the first pain. As the pains became stronger and more frequent, I decided to wake Frank, and then I called Dr. Benoit, who told us to meet him at the hospital.

Frank and I had our own thoughts as we took a taxi to St. Boniface Hospital. My heart was full of joy at the thought of a baby, but I wished that my parents could be with us to welcome their first grandchild.

At the same time, I knew Frank must have been thinking of the responsibility he was facing with a new member in the family.

After we arrived and registered, and I was settled comfortably in my room, the nurse told Frank to go into the waiting room while she examined me.

"You just relax while we put your wife to work. We'll let you know the minute the baby arrives."

Frank took me in his arms. "I'll be with you all the way, honey. Remember, I love you."

I had an easy delivery. When the doctor laid the tiny baby in my arms, I forgot all the discomfort as I looked at my son. He was red and wrinkled, and had a lot of dark hair. My heart filled with love for my tiny baby.

When I was back in my room, Frank came in. I'll never forget his expression when he looked at me. "Oh, Terrie, I've just seen our son. He'll be a wonderful football player. Did you see the size of his hands?"

Our baby was very long and weighed almost seven pounds.

"I'm sorry I didn't give you a daughter. Are you disappointed?"

"Terrie, honey, I have the only girl I ever want right here in my arms." He kissed me. "Now, we have to decide on a boy's name. What do you think of Brock?" Frank said. "I read a book by an author named Brock Saunders and I really like that name."

"That sounds good to me. Let's use Allen, too. I'd like to have my family included."

"Allen Brock Dagg sounds perfect."

Brock arrived on July 30, 1947, and four days later, Frank and I took him home. Life couldn't get much better. We had a son, a new house and Frank had a job.

Brock was a happy baby. Frank and I played with him for hours each day. I longed for my family to see Brock.

One day, Frank came home with a surprise. "Guess what?" he announced. "I'm getting a bonus and I'll be going on day work soon. I want you to use the bonus money to take Brock to see his grandfather."

I threw myself into Frank's arms. "Oh, Frank, that would be wonderful, but can we really afford it? We could use your bonus for other things we need."

"Well, dear, there's a right time for everything, and I feel it's important for you to see your family. Besides, I want to show off our son."

Early in May, 1948, Brock and I boarded a plane bound for England. Frank held us both in his arms at the airport. "Have a wonderful time and take care. I'll miss you both. Give my love to everyone and tell them I'll bring you myself next time."

Chapter 7

The flight to England was pleasant and ten-month-old Brock slept much of the time. When the plane landed in Montreal to refuel, I remembered when I'd arrived there from England in 1944.

When the big four-engine plane landed at London's Heathrow airport, I bought a train ticket to Nottingham. Then I took Brock for his first train ride. My heart pounded as the conductor called, "Nottingham."

As I stepped onto the platform, I saw my dad with Marjorie and Bill hurrying toward us. "Hello, dear," Dad said as he took Brock and me in his arms. Brock gave his grandfather a great big smile.

"He's beautiful," Marjorie said as she held Brock. "Kathleen and Phil are at home with Richard. Kathleen's anxious for you to see your nephew." Kathleen's little boy, Richard, was two months old.

I was disturbed to see the change in Dad. He'd aged. When we arrived at the bungalow Dad shared with Kathleen and Phil, Kathleen ran out to meet us. "Richard's sleeping and Phil's not home yet, but I have tea ready. My, Brock is such a big boy."

The family reunion was wonderful. Kathleen and I were a little stilted toward each other at first, remembering our last conversation. However, before long, we were more at ease. Much had happened since 1944 and we had to put the past behind us.

When Phil arrived home, he greeted me with a kiss before picking Brock up. "My, what a big boy. He'll be walking before his first birthday."

We heard sounds from Richard's room. Kathleen said, "Terrie, let's take Brock to meet his cousin."

Richard was an adorable baby, fair-haired with light blue eyes and the typical creamy complexion of English youngsters. He smiled and gurgled in my arms. Kathleen told Brock he could touch the baby. Brock seemed fascinated. When I saw the two babies together, I realized why Phil remarked how big Brock seemed. Next to his tiny two-month-old cousin, he really was a big boy. I said later, "Oh, Kathleen, how mother would have loved her grandsons."

The visit in England was wonderful. I took Brock to see Edith as soon as I had an opportunity. The old lady's eyes were full of love as she sat with Brock on her knee.

"It seems such a short time since you were a baby, Terrie. He's a beautiful boy. You look so well. Frank must make you very happy."

"Oh, Edith, I just wish mother could have lived to see how happy we are and to see her grandsons."

"I guess it was not meant to be, dear. We don't decide those things. Are you keeping up with your dancing as you promised?"

I confessed that I'd been busy with the house and the baby. "Sometimes I dance to the radio. I still find it very hard to sit still when I hear music. I promise to make an effort to practice more."

The peacetime Y was quite different from when I'd worked there. Mamie was no longer working, but Madge and Richie were still in the office, and Jim Edgar was still manager. They were delighted to see me and to play with Brock. They were also interested in hearing about my life in Canada. I remembered the night of the surprise party and knew that these were the friends who had made my life with Frank possible.

After a couple of weeks, I began to feel very homesick for Frank. I missed him more than I'd thought I would. Every night seemed longer, every day emptier. When Brock would do something new, I tried to be content, enjoy my family, but I longed for Frank to share it with me. I wondered how I'd manage to stay for three months.

On July 30th, Brock had his first birthday. Kathleen had a party with all of the family and Edith. Brock blew out the candle on his cake.

When the time came to leave, Dad and Kathleen took Brock and me to the station to catch the train to London. Marjorie and Bill brought Edith. Smiling through my tears as I said goodbye, I promised them all I'd try to return again soon. Next time Frank would come, too.

I took Kathleen aside. "Dad looks tired. He really doesn't seem too well. Maybe you could persuade him to get a checkup."

"It's not easy to get him to a doctor, but I'll try."

When I hugged Bill and Marjorie goodbye, they promised they would come to visit us in Canada. They ran a successful business manufacturing house dresses and aprons, and they had built a lovely bungalow in Nottingham. They had no children.

Finally, I hugged my father. "Daddy, I know you're wondering why I didn't visit mother's grave. You see, I want to remember her as she was when we lived in the old house where I grew up. If I see the grave, I'll just take unhappy memories home with me.

"I understand, dear. Now, you must promise to take care of yourself and my grandson. Tell Frank he's welcome any time, so try to come as soon as you can."

I watched from the train window until my family was out of sight. I wondered if I'd ever see my dear old nurse again.

I was excited when I realized that in a few hours Brock and I would be with Frank again. By coming to England, I'd made peace with my family and resolved some of my anxieties from my mother's death.

The flight to Winnipeg was uneventful. Brock behaved well. The passengers were helpful in amusing him on the long journey. I was grateful he was such a friendly little boy.

Dad had given Brock a handsome Harris Tweed coat before we left England, and Edith had knitted matching berets for Brock and me. They were oatmeal-colored angora wool.

Brock had grown while we'd been gone. He looked like a little man holding my hand as we walked from the plane. I could see Frank waiting, so I let Brock go and watched as he walked steadily to his daddy. What a surprise for Frank.

Tears ran down my cheeks.

"What a big boy! Where is the little baby I sent off to

England?" Frank said. We hugged with Brock in between us. "Every day was so empty, every night so lonely. Please, don't ever leave me alone again, Terrie."

"Don't worry," I said. "I never knew three months could last so long. It was important that I took Brock to see my family, but we belong together and that's how it'll be from now on."

That evening at home, after Brock was in bed, I showed Frank the pictures of our visit with my family in England.

We were both grateful that we had resolved the problems of the past.

The next few years were happy for the Dagg family. Frank and I enjoyed watching Brock grow into a husky boy. He was a favorite with his aunts and uncles. Tony, now seven, and Derek, five, came to the house often. Brock loved to play with his older cousins.

I was surprised one day, two years later, when I sorted the mail and found a letter from a solicitor in England. The letter informed me I'd been left a small inheritance from my grandfather that was to be given to me when I turned twenty-five. I didn't remember my grandfather because he'd died when I was a baby. When I told Frank, he said, "Well, honey, I think you should leave the money in England and we'll just have to go over there to pick it up."

I could hardly believe my ears. "Frank, are you kidding me?"

"How about having Christmas with your family this year?" Franks eyes were sparkling with excitement. I was absolutely stunned, but also grateful for this chance to see my family, again.

"I've given it some thought, and I believe your family would be happy to have us. I can get passes for the train trip to Nova

Scotia and a discount on the boat fare. Your inheritance will take care of the expenses in England. How about it?"

We wrote to the family at once and received a reply telling us how wonderful it would be to have us. Kathleen and Phil wanted us to stay with them. Richard was three and would love to have his cousin for the holidays.

In late November 1950, I wondered if I was pregnant again. A visit to Dr. Benoit confirmed my suspicion.

"You'll have a new family member in mid-June," he said. "The trip to England won't be a problem. The sea air will be good for you."

I decided not to tell Frank. The news would be a wonderful Christmas gift for him, and I could give my family a surprise, too.

We took the train to Nova Scotia. Three-year-old Brock enjoyed every minute of the ride. His eyes were like saucers when he saw the big ocean liner that would take us to England.

The voyage was wonderful. The Cunard ships are elegant, which makes a cruise seem almost like living in a wonderland. The seas weren't rough and Brock kept amused in the area where he could play with other children. We had a Christmas party on board the ship before we docked in Liverpool.

Still, I couldn't help but remember my last cruise when I sailed on the Queen Mary under very different circumstances. An eternity seemed to have passed since that voyage. Now, instead of a young girl, I was a wife and mother.

As we boarded the train to Nottingham, Frank said, "Terrie, the sea air must agree with you. You look radiant and I think you've gained a little weight."

The whole family met us at Victoria Station. Kathleen and Phil looked the same as I remembered from three years earlier.

Richard was a handsome little boy. Brock was still tall for his age. The boys became friends at once.

Marjorie and Bill looked older. Bill was heavier than I remembered, but Marjorie was the same as always with her warm, sincere smile. She had always been a good friend to me.

Dad did not look as strong as he had three years before. I could tell he'd lost weight. He gave me a big hug and kiss, and told me how happy he was to see us again, especially his grandson. Brock went to his grandfather right away, and proceeded to tell him about the train ride and the big boat trip.

"How is Edith?" I asked Marjorie.

"I know you'll want to see her, so she'll be with us for Christmas. She can hardly wait to see you."

The family welcomed Frank as if the past had never happened. The one thing that marred the perfect Christmas was Mom's absence.

Edith arrived with Bill and Marjorie on Christmas day. She looked wonderful, although a little frail at eighty-four. She still wore her white hair in a bun. She had lost a little height, but her back was straight and her skin was pale with only a few wrinkles. Her blue eyes lit up when she smiled. She still had the kind face I'll always remember from my childhood.

My eyes filled with tears as I went into her arms. We held each other as the years slipped away and we reminisced about the times we'd spent together in the kitchen of the old house, both of us shedding happy tears.

"What a perfect Christmas," she said, as she gave Brock a big hug. "Family is so important in our lives. It's wonderful to have everyone together."

Kathleen had set the table with her lovely English china, sterling silver, damask cloth and napkins, and the traditional, colorful crackers. The boys loved pulling the crackers open to find a little toy and a paper hat inside.

We enjoyed talking about our lives and the things that had happened since we'd been apart, especially the difference between life in Winnipeg and that in Nottingham. Everyone agreed the miles that separated us would not keep us from being close to each other.

My thoughts went back to the Christmases we had shared as children — the pillow cases Kathleen and I found at the foot of our beds on Christmas morning, and when Mom took us to the Children's Hospital so we could give the children little presents. Mom always said this was to teach us to not be selfish and to know how fortunate we were.

As we sat around the Christmas table, Dad carved the turkey and we each filled our plates with a wonderful array of food — turkey, stuffing, mashed potatoes, green beans, cranberry sauce and gravy. Before we began to eat, Frank stood up.

"I would like to say grace and give thanks to God for allowing us all to be together for His birthday. I pray He'll allow everyone to enjoy good health and happiness in the years to come."

We sat in silence for a few moments, each with our own thoughts.

Brock and Richard were anxious to play with their toys from Santa, so we allowed them to leave the table while we adults had our traditional English Christmas Pudding with custard. Then we relaxed in the living room with our tea or coffee.

I decided that would be a good time to make my announcement. I took Frank's hand and said, "I won't be able to give you your Christmas present until June. I did bring it with me, but you'll have to wait until the middle of June to welcome your new son or daughter."

Frank was speechless. He took me in his arms, finally, and said, "How could you ever keep such a secret? Now I know why you've been so happy the last few months."

Everyone was surprised and delighted with my announcement. Dad gave me a big hug and told me I should have his third grandchild on his birthday. "I'll be sixty-three on June thirteenth," he said.

I told him I would do my best. Since Brock was born a couple of days early, maybe this baby would come ahead of schedule also.

Edith was very happy. She told me she would start knitting right away. "It will be so good for Brock to have a brother or sister."

Frank and I told the family that they must try to come to Winnipeg. We wanted them to meet Frank's brothers and sisters, and to see our house and the area we lived in. I felt strongly about my family seeing how well Frank had done and how happy our marriage was.

The next day, Frank and I left Brock playing with Richard so we could visit the Y together. The boys club was filled with youngsters now, not servicemen and volunteers. Jim and Rosemary Edgar had retired and a new office staff had taken the place of Richie and Madge. Frank told me he wanted to ask one of the boys to have a game of chess with him, just for old time's sake.

When the time came to say our goodbyes to the family, we decided it would be easier at Kathleen and Phil's house, rather than at the train station. Kathleen promised to try to come for a visit before long.

Just before we left, Frank took me to see Edith. I knew it'd probably be the last time I'd see my devoted old nanny. Edith looked at me and knew what was going through my mind. "Don't you feel sad, dear. I've lived a long and happy life. Most of my happiness is because of you. You have made me so proud. I know you'll return to your dancing one day."

I tried to hold back my tears as Edith said, "You have a lovely little boy and soon you'll have a new member of your family. Frank is a wonderful husband. I know he'll always be good to you. Terrie, I could not love you more if you were my own child."

I held Edith in my arms, as if our roles were reversed. Now, I should take care of Edith. I felt guilty as I left because I was aware that Marjorie was doing the job that really was mine. However, I knew my place was with Frank and my own little family. I gave Edith one more kiss, and then didn't look back as we left her apartment.

I couldn't stop myself from thinking about all that had happened since that day in 1944 when I stood on the platform of Victoria Station, headed for Canada and a new life. I knew I had done what I had to do, but I felt so sad that my mother didn't live to see how happy Frank and I were together. Why couldn't she have faced me instead of letting Bill hit me and accuse me of things that weren't true. And why did she let Kathleen speak such unkind words to me, and plan Kathleen's wedding right across the street from the Y where I worked and not invite or include me.

If only Mother had tried to talk and reason with me instead of making everyone in the family push me away by being so unkind. I know Frank and I would have waited until the war was over before marrying, if only she had treated me with love and understanding.

Before we went to the train station, I asked Kathleen to persuade Dad to see a doctor. "He looks so old and tired. I noticed he seems to be in pain when he walks and seems to hold his chest at times. He told me the doctors had prescribed nitroglycerine pills. He obviously has angina."

"I'll try to persuade him. He's planning a trip to France in March. Maybe that'll help him."

As I kissed Dad, I promised him, "I'll really try to have this baby on June thirteen, but you have to promise me to come see us."

As we boarded the same Cunard ship we had sailed on a few weeks earlier, Frank and I both felt satisfied we had made peace with my family. Frank told me over and over how glad he was that we made the trip so my family could see that we had a good marriage.

Our journey wasn't as pleasant as our trip over. We encountered five days of heavy seas in the Atlantic Ocean. Most of the passengers were seasick, including Frank and me.

Thank goodness Brock didn't seem to be affected by the storm and rolling seas. He played in the children's nursery and insisted I watch him ride on the carousel in the nursery with its brightly colored horses. That was not a lot of fun.

Everyone was glad when the ship docked. Frank and I hurried ashore to catch our train to Winnipeg. The train ride was pleasant after the rough sea voyage. The next morning, we called

Lydia to let her know we were home. She was excited to hear all our news. She asked about my family, how did they like Brock and had things changed in England since the wartime.

Once her questions ended, and I had a chance to talk, I told her that my dad may come over in June to meet his third grandchild. Lydia only took a few seconds to catch on to what I'd just said. "Are you telling me you'll be having another baby in June?"

"Yes."

Lydia then announced that she wanted the baby to be born on her birthday, June 17. "It would be a great birthday present."

I told her I couldn't promise anything since I felt the baby had a mind of its own. "Besides, I promised Dad to try to give him a birthday present on June thirteen, his birthday." I laughed. "I just hope the baby'll cooperate with at least one of you."

I had no problem with my pregnancy. When I went for my routine checkup in late May, Dr. Benoit told me the baby would probably arrive in mid-June. I felt wonderful as I walked home holding Brock's hand. He was a sensitive and sweet little boy.

Frank and I talked with Brock and explained that a baby was coming. He was anxious to see his new brother or sister.

I was working in the kitchen when the telegram arrived. Luckily, Frank was home. He took the yellow envelope from me and took me in his arms. His face was white as he read the message.

"You don't have to tell me, Frank. My father's gone, isn't he?"

Frank handed me the wire. "Dad died of a heart attack June 8, 1951. Details later. Kathleen."

I thought my heart would stop. I couldn't talk. The tears didn't come until I felt Frank's arms holding me tight. I'm sure he thought my heart was going to break.

"Why, Frank? Why did this have to happen? Am I being punished for what I did to Mom and Dad? I never meant to hurt anyone. I just wanted to be with you. Was I selfish? Am I a really bad person?"

Frank's arms felt so comforting. He said, "Don't blame yourself, honey. We don't decide when we live or die. That's God's decision."

"It's too late for me to give Dad his birthday present. There's no point in my going to England now, even if Dr. Benoit would let me travel."

A letter from Kathleen arrived a few days later telling us that Dad had died of a coronary attack while visiting cousins in Grantham. He'd collapsed in the bedroom and was dead when they found him. The funeral had been small. He was buried beside Mom.

On June 16, Jonathan Kent Dagg arrived. He was a beautiful baby, fair-skinned with blond hair and dark blue eyes. He looked very content as the nurse handed him to me. He entered the world without any difficulty and I was sure he'd arrived with an inquiring look on his face. He weighed exactly seven pounds, not as long as Brock had been but chubbier, and he had blond hair. They did not look at all alike.

Frank came to the room grinning from ear to ear. "Isn't he wonderful, honey? I can hardly wait for Brock to see him."

Although Kent was not born on either his grandfather's or Aunt Lydia's birthday, he did manage to be born on Father's Day, 1951.

When Frank and I brought his baby brother home, Brock said, "I thought he'd be bigger so we could play together."

Not long after Kent was born, Marjorie wrote that Edith's health was failing. "She seems to be sleeping a lot and getting more confused and frail. Don't worry, I'll keep a close watch and let you know how things are."

In the meantime, Frank became restless at his job. He found the work monotonous and boring. I wasn't surprised when he came home one day and said, "Terrie, how would you feel about taking another crack at California." By now, Brock was almost five and Kent, twelve months.

I stopped stirring the stew on the stove, put my arms around him, and said, "You know I'll go with your plans, but this time we have two little boys to consider, so we must make it work. They need to have stability in their lives."

Like many married couples, Frank and I had our disagreements, but we always got things solved before we said goodnight. Frank was very easygoing. He had an infectious sense of humor. Arguing with him was mostly futile as I always ended up the loser and laughing about it later.

"It would mean selling the house and starting all over again. I'm thirty-five and if I don't do it soon, I'll be too old. My plan is to go to Minneapolis and pick up a good used car and a motorhome. They build really nice ones, now. We could use it as our home in California until we get established."

"Wow, you must have been thinking about this for a long time," I said. "I'm sure you'll be able to get a job this time."

"I'd like to try the San Francisco area instead of Los Angeles. I still intend to build our boat and sail on San Francisco Bay."

My mind was in a whirl as I listened to Frank's plans. I

remembered how hard it had been a few years before. However, I knew how much Frank wanted to be close to the ocean. He had never stopped hoping to build our boat. It seemed my life would never settle down, but Frank was right. If we waited much longer, it would be too late to get established in a new country.

In my heart, I knew Frank was a dreamer. That was one of the things I loved most about him. He had so much drive and imagination that life was never dull.

We looked forward to the move. We were to begin a new life in America. Frank liked the Palo Alto area, south of San Francisco. We learned that the city had good schools, which was important to us since Brock would be starting kindergarten soon after we arrived.

The next weeks were hectic. We sold our house to the second couple who looked at it. They paid the asking price, so Frank and I made a nice profit from our little home in Norwood.

As planned, Frank went to Minneapolis to buy a car as prices were much cheaper than in Canada. He returned a few days later with a 1949 Pontiac pulling a 28' motorhome.

I fell in love with our new home as soon as I looked inside. The motorhome had a bedroom in the back with a double bed and built-in drawers, perfect for the boys. There was a dinette with upholstered seats that made into a bed Frank and I would share. The kitchen had a small stove and refrigerator, and an amazing amount of cupboard space. Our new home even had a tiny bathroom. Brock wanted to sleep in the motor home the night his daddy brought it home.

Our neighbors were curious, and as I let them walk through the motorhome, Frank remarked, "We should charge admission. It'd help pay for our trip."

Because of the weather in Winnipeg, motorhomes were unheard of, so ours was a novelty. The family was impressed and although they hated to see Frank take his family so far away, they all agreed we were making a good move.

"I'd do it myself, if I were younger," Pud said. "The winters here get worse every year and besides, you'll have a hard time getting a job in the states if you wait much longer."

Frank and I didn't have a problem getting our passports. This time we had enough money and didn't need a sponsor. The evening before we left Winnipeg, Maude had a family party. Having everyone there was great. Frank's family had been so caring, never judging me for the way I'd left my family in England. I also hoped we wouldn't regret our decision to leave them. I also hoped we weren't making a mistake, but I told myself that this time all would be well.

Derek and Tony were unhappy to say goodbye to their cousins, but I told them what a wonderful time they'd have when their parents brought them to visit us in California.

"I'll miss you all so much," I told everyone, "but Frank deserves his chance to try again. I know we'll have better luck this time."

As we drove out of Winnipeg early the next morning, I wondered what lay ahead. Much had happened since leaving England eight years before. Both of my parents had died, I had two fine sons, Frank and I had sold two houses and now we were starting all over again, this time in a strange country with no family or friends.

Leaving was especially hard for me. I was giving up a family for the second time. I really wanted the boys to have

aunts and uncles and cousins since they would never know
grandparents. I rationalized that everyone would visit us in
America once we were settled. I knew Frank would never he
happy until he was closer to the Pacific Ocean so he could build
his boat. Even though that dream seemed a long way off, we had
to try to make the dream a reality.

Kent, 7, and Brock, 11, fishing at Lake Brereton in Manitoba, Canada

Brock, high school graduation 1965.

Kent, high school graduation 1969.

Frank's dream was really beginning to come true. He still had no power tools. It was truly a labor of love.

A lot more work to do yet. My childhood friend, Keith Bass, was visiting from England. He was impressed.

Chapter 8

The trip to California was a wonderful experience. Our car was reliable and the trailer parks where we stayed each night were in magnificent scenic areas.

Brock and Kent were good travelers. They napped each day. I let them play outside in the evenings to get some exercise before giving them showers and reading to them at bedtime. Frank and I enjoyed a few hours alone, but we'd go to bed early so we'd be fresh for the next day of our journey.

Frank had decided we would try to find a motorhome park in Palo Alto, a small college town about 33 miles south of San Francisco. Stanford University is a famous landmark in Palo Alto. We were impressed when we read about it in our travel guide.

As we got closer to San Francisco, Frank elected to go straight through the city. We could always explore San Francisco after we were settled and not pulling a motorhome.

I could hardly believe my eyes when I saw San Francisco Bay. It took my breath away. I had never seen anything so beautiful. The sun was shining on the gorgeous blue water that was dotted with dozens of sailboats gliding gracefully across the Bay. I was beginning to understand Frank's love for sailing and I, too, wanted to build our boat and sail on this bay.

The Golden Gate Bridge was unlike anything I'd ever seen, big and impressive as it spanned the Bay from Sausalito to the San Francisco skyline on the horizon. Shining in the sun, the bridge looked truly golden. "I've never seen anything like this in England or Canada," I told Frank. "One day I'd like to walk across this bridge."

"See that other bridge?" Frank said. "It goes from Oakland to San Francisco. One day we'll sail under both those bridges."

We were awed as Frank drove through the City. The hills and heavy traffic challenged us. But, Frank was a good driver.

We picked up highway 101 out of the City, then drove south on El Camino Real heading toward our future home. We noticed how many small towns we passed along the way, each one blending into the next.

As we drove, I was thinking that it would be a long time before we'd be able to build our boat. Frank had to find work, we had to find a house, and we had to raise our sons before we could even consider a boat. However, I hadn't lost faith that the day would come.

When we drove into Palo Alto, we spotted a group of buildings on the right side with a very impressive clock tower and beautiful landscaping. "That must be Stanford University," Frank said. "We'll have to walk around the campus once we're settled."

We stopped at a service station to ask the attendant if he could direct us to a place where we could park our motorhome.

The attendant said there was nothing like that in Palo Alto, but there was an excellent one in Mountain View, a few miles south, named Roll-In Trailer Manor. Since we had a motorhome, not a trailer, I hoped the place would be okay.

Frank followed the directions and soon spotted the sign in Mountain View. The park, lovely with big trees, a lawn and a restroom for each space, was situated right on El Camino Real. I waited anxiously while Frank went to the office.

Frank was smiling as he came back to the car. "We're all set, honey. We have space twenty-five and I paid the rent for two months."

We got the motorhome leveled in no time. After washing up in our new private bathroom, Frank said, "I think we should celebrate by having dinner out tonight. First thing tomorrow, I start job hunting."

Our evening was joyous. The boys loved the park. We were so glad to be staying in one place for a while. "I just know things will go well here," Frank said. "Terrie, I love you so much and I'm so grateful for the confidence you have in me. Not many women would have given up their security to take a gamble like this."

"I don't think it's a gamble, Frank. If we work at it together, everything will be fine." Actually, I did agree with him.

Frank left the next morning full of confidence. I put Kent in his stroller and Brock pushed his brother as we explored the park. I was looking for the laundry room when I met a young woman walking with a boy about Brock's age.

"Hi," I said. "We're new here. Would you like to join me for a cup of coffee?"

The woman smiled. "I'd love to. We just arrived here from Boston." She told me her husband was a television repairman and he was looking for a job. "My name's Edie Davis and this is Jack. He's four years old," she said.

As Edie and I got acquainted, Brock and Jack played with their cars and Kent watched from his playpen. I wondered if I should find out where to enroll Brock in kindergarten.

"I've been wondering about that, too," Edie said. "Maybe the manager can tell us where the nearest school is."

The manager directed us to a school within walking distance, so we decided to go right over there. I put Kent back in his stroller, and Jack and Brock ran ahead as Edie and I enjoyed the walk to the school.

We were able to register the boys for kindergarten classes on September 8, just four days away.

When Frank came home, he was all smiles. "Guess what? You're now looking at an appliance salesman." He explained that he was in Montgomery Ward in Palo Alto, looking at television sets and talking to the manager. When Frank told him we had just arrived and he was looking for a job, the manager said he was looking for a salesman.

"It's not exactly the kind of work I was planning, but the opportunity of having a job right away was too good to turn down. I'll have to work on Saturdays and Thursday evenings, but it's a start. I would have preferred to get a job flying." With his hearing problem, that wasn't possible.

"Well, I've had a busy day, too." I told him about my new friend and getting Brock registered for kindergarten.

"You see, dear," Frank said, "things are working out for us this time. I just know we made the right move."

We were a happy couple putting our two boys to bed that night.

One Sunday, a few weeks after we got settled, Frank took us for a drive. We noticed a housing development in nearby Sunnyvale, a small town of 4,400 people south of Palo Alto. The area was surrounded by fruit orchards. Pear, apricot and cherry trees filled the countryside for miles on the outskirts of the town. We were amazed at all the new building in the area.

The development was called Cherry Chase. We decided to go through the model homes. They all had a similar floor plan. Some were reversed. They had three bedrooms, one bath, a big living room with space for a dining area, and a nice kitchen with an eating area. Large windows ran along the entire back wall of the living room that looked out onto the garden.

Frank was impressed with the quality of the materials and the workmanship. He informed me we should have a two car garage. I had to laugh. "We can hardly afford the house, so when do you think we'll be able to afford two cars?"

The salesman, who had overheard our conversation, told us that the next group of houses would be a little larger and would have two car garages.

"The houses will be completed in about six months. Where do you live now?"

When Frank told him, the man seemed very interested. "My brother and his wife just retired and are looking for a motorhome to do some traveling. Would you be interested in selling?"

"Well, we hadn't really thought about it, but they're welcome to look at ours."

Frank gave the salesman our address and in return, Mr. Henderson, the salesman, gave Frank his business card with his brother's name written on the back.

As we left, Frank said, "I doubt if we'll ever see or hear from his brother, but you never know."

I had a feeling, as we drove home to the park, one day we'd be living in Cherry Chase.

The following Thursday night, as I put Kent to bed, I heard a tap on the door. Brock ran to answer, with me following after him. I opened the door to find an elderly couple.

"We're the Hendersons. My brother's a real estate salesman and he mentioned you might be interested in selling your motorhome."

I explained that Frank wasn't home, but they were welcome to look around.

The Henderson's were a friendly couple and they were impressed with the motorhome. Mrs. Henderson said, "This is a much roomier home than I imagined. It's well planned."

"If you would like to come back another night when my husband is home, he can tell you more about the technical things than I can."

"Well, we're certainly interested in buying if the price is right. Would tomorrow evening be okay to come back?"

I could hardly wait for Frank to come home. When I told him about the Henderson's, he was really happy. He told me things were going to work out so we could buy a house in Cherry Chase. We'd need to sell the motorhome for at least $2500 in order to have the down payment.

When the Hendersons arrived at 7:30 the next evening, I had coffee and dessert waiting for them.

Mr. Henderson told Frank he'd sign an agreement the following Monday evening and pay with a cashier's check.

After the Hendersons left, I said, "Frank, what a wonderful coincidence this has been. I'm so happy."

Frank found a house to rent in Palo Alto and put the down payment money in the bank. I had a small inheritance from my father, so I was able to buy a living room couch and chair, plus a few other things for our new home.

The Hendersons offered the use of their truck to move us to our rented house. My entire life in England had been spent in one house and as I looked around our temporary home, I wondered if I'd ever be settled in one place. In a few years, I had lived in three houses and a motorhome in three countries. Now, we'd be renting a house as we waited for what I hoped would be our home for many years. Little did I know I'd live at 1259 Susan Way in Sunnyvale for 49 years.

Every Sunday, Frank and I would take the boys for a ride and stop at Cherry Chase to check on the construction of the model we had picked out. The lot we'd chosen had five apricot trees, two in the front and three in the back. What would we do with all that fruit?

I began to select colors for the kitchen, and the tile and linoleum for the bathroom. The house, only 1,000 square feet, had three bedrooms and a large living room. The master bedroom was so large, Frank said we could add a half bath one day. I told Frank he was really becoming Americanized. First he had to have a two car garage, and now he was thinking about two bathrooms.

We were comfortable in the rented house, but Christmas 1952 was a strange one for us. We were not used to having such warm weather for the holiday. I took the boys to see Santa Claus at Macy's and we bought a tiny, live Christmas tree. We were lonely that Christmas, but we had each other and the promise of moving to our own house made up for not having family around. We were happy as we thanked God before opening our gifts and enjoying a turkey dinner.

In April 1953, the day finally arrived. Frank and I were given a move-in day of May 1. As we loaded our furniture on a rented truck, we realized how much more we'd need to furnish our new home.

"We have plenty of time. We'll just have to go slow, Terrie," Frank said.

"First we need drapes for those big living room windows," I said. "The windows with blinds can wait and I can make the kitchen curtains."

"We have to put up a fence between our neighbor's houses. I think they'll share the cost of the side fences," Frank said. "Thank goodness the builder will put a fence across the back."

"Well, Frank," I said. "Since we finally own our house, I think we should plan to stay for a while. I think we've found the perfect place to raise our family."

I was right. One by one, the new houses were occupied by young families. The new school was not yet complete, so Brock had to attend an older school on the other side of Sunnyvale. One day, when I took him to the bus stop to catch the school bus, I met a woman about my age holding a toddler by the hand. She was putting a little girl on the bus who looked about Brock's age. I introduced myself and asked if she would like to have a cup of coffee. "It'd be nice to get to know some of my neighbors."

That was the beginning of a lifelong friendship. Shirley and Howard Berry had two daughters. Susie was five and Laurie 15 months, the same ages as Brock and Kent. They'd bought a house a few houses down on the opposite side of the street. Both of them were native Californians. Howard, a pilot, flew with Pan Am.

Later that night, when I told Frank about Shirley, my new friend, I noticed a little envy in Frank's voice as he said, "Howard's job is one I'd give my right arm for."

Chapter 9

As the months flew by, the house became a home. Frank and I had wonderful neighbors, especially Howard and Shirley. Howard was away a lot, so I often spent evenings keeping Shirley company. We had a lot in common. I became a den mother for Brock's Cub Scout group, and Frank became a coach for one of the local Little League Baseball teams.

Life was busy and happy, except for the growing need for extra money. It seemed that we were living from one paycheck to the next. Groceries were getting more expensive and the boys ate more and more as they grew older.

I decided it was time for me to help out. I remembered Edith telling me that one day my dancing would be useful to me. I decided this might be the time.

Each day I disciplined myself to practice for an hour. I discovered I hadn't forgotten any of my training. In a few weeks,

I'd brushed up on my ballet steps and terminology. The tap steps and acrobatics were easy to pick up again.

One evening in 1955, after I'd put the boys to bed, I approached Frank with my idea.

"I'm going to try to rent space in the shopping center to start a children's dance school and teach two hours a day. I want to stay home on Saturday to be with you and the boys.

"It sounds wonderful, honey," he said, "but don't you think you have enough to do with the house, the boys and all your other interests? Maybe I should try to find a second job. I've been trying to get an interview with one of the new electronic companies." Frank was still worried because of his age and his lack of a college degree.

"I really want to give my idea a try," I said. "I don't want to see you take on two jobs. It's important for the boys to be with you as often as possible."

The next day, I went to the nearby shopping center and located the business office across the street. I asked the secretary who I should talk to about renting space. She directed me to a small office and introduced me to an older gentleman.

"This is Mr. Arnold, the owner and builder of the center."

The gray-haired manager smiled. "Please sit down, young lady. What can I do for you?"

I explained what I had in mind. I needed an empty space with bare walls for practice bars and mirrors, and a restroom.

Mr. Arnold agreed that my idea of a children's dancing school made sense as there were so many new families in the community. He reminded me that I would need liability insurance. I told him I would only be teaching ten children in each class as I had a family who needed me, also.

"I think I have what you need. Come on over to the shopping center."

We left the office and walked across the street to a shoe repair store in the shopping center. Mr. Arnold talked to the owners of the business and asked permission for us to walk through to the rear of the store. There, we found empty floor space with a door leading to a back entrance.

"If I arranged to have a partition between the shoe repair area and this space, would that be enough room for you?" Mr. Arnold continued. "You could use this back door as an entrance to your dance studio and share the restroom with the shoe repair renters.

"This would be perfect," I said.

Mr. Arnold invited me to join him for a cup of coffee and then surprised me when he said, "Terrie, I've always admired people with enthusiasm and determination. I'm going to charge eighty dollars a month for the space and as long as I run this center, I'll never raise your rent. We'll sign a contract to that effect."

I felt like hugging him, but I shook his hand instead and told him I'd like to open the school on May 1st.

That night, Frank and I talked for hours about the plans I had for my dance school. Frank said he'd install the mirror and practice bars. We decided to use the big mirror from our bedroom to save money. I made flyers to announce the opening of Terrie's School of Dance. The following day, I asked for permission from the principal of Cherry Chase School to allow Brock to distribute the flyers to each classroom. Then, I arranged for an open house the first Sunday in April. I asked Shirley, plus two other friends, to help serve tea and cookies. We welcomed mothers and their children to the school. By the end of the day, 65 children had enrolled in Terrie's School of Dance.

I wrote Edith right away to tell her the exciting news. I was finally doing what my nanny had always wanted. My letter crossed with one from Kathleen telling me that Edith had passed away. The sweet old lady had apparently died in her sleep. I was devastated. I felt such a terrible loss. The kind and unselfish woman had devoted so much of her life to me, taking me to my dancing lessons, giving me advice, always being there to listen to my problems. Her love and wisdom had been invaluable to me. "I'll make a success of the school and somehow Edith will know," I told Frank that night as we lay close before falling asleep.

The school was a joy for me. Each afternoon, Brock would mind Kent for an hour until Frank got home. Shirley was always available, if necessary. The school was only a five minute walk from the house, so I wasn't nervous about the boys.

Very soon my classes were filled and I had 100 students ranging from ages four to fourteen. Some students had more dancing ability and coordination than others, but all were anxious to learn.

Several months later, I began rehearsing for our first recital. I got permission to use the stage at Cherry Chase School. The mothers helped with the costumes. I made a few of the tutus and arranged for the programs. I asked friends to help with the children backstage during the performance.

The recital went well and was truly rewarding for me. I'd worked hard and so had the children. This was the first of many successful recitals I directed and produced for my students.

By the end of the year, I had all the students I could handle, plus a waiting list of prospective students, so I hired a young teacher to assist me.

In 1957, Frank and I took a night school course to prepare for our American citizenship exam. We'd lived in the United States almost five years and were eligible to apply. We had to have two people act as witnesses for us who we'd known for at least five years. Shirley and Howard had been transferred to Connecticut, so I asked our friends and neighbors, Edith and Larry McFarlane, to accompany us.

On the day of the test, Frank, Edith, Larry and I drove to San Francisco. I was very nervous. I did well answering the questions until the last examiner asked me what the Board of Supervisors was and what were the duties of the members.

"I really don't know," I said.

"Well, you go home and study and try again next month," the official said.

I was crushed. As we drove home, Frank told me not to worry. "That wasn't a fair question, dear. The Board of Supervisors is a city organization. I doubt if many Americans know the members' duties."

Edith and Larry agreed. "You did fine, Terrie. You'll pass next time. That examiner must have been in a bad mood. He didn't give you a chance."

I was a little bitter when I went back to San Francisco the next month. I felt I was already a good citizen—a Cub Scout leader, a PTA member, a successful small business owner. When I passed the test that time, I felt much better. Now, I had a right to vote and speak my mind. I was no longer just a visitor in the United States, but truly a part of the country.

My school was very successful. Each year a large crowd attended the recital. I let some of the children pass through the audience during the intermission to collect money to be donated

to the Stanford Children's Hospital. I often thought how proud
my nanny, Edith, would have been to see how many children I
taught to dance and how much they enjoyed performing. Because
of Edith, and her encouragement, I had created a thriving dance
school.

The summers were busy. I had my school, and Frank
worked hard with his Little League players. Brock showed signs
of becoming an adept athlete. Kent was not as well-coordinated
as his older brother, but he was a happy youngster, very easy
going and full of fun. I wished many times my parents could have
lived to see their grandsons grow up.

Frank finally landed a job with Hewlett-Packard, the
company he had wanted to work for. "I'll have to work at night
for awhile, but I'm so happy to get a job with Hewlett-Packard.
I'll work any hours they want me to. I hope to get on a day shift,
eventually."

In 1962, Frank asked me how I felt about starting to build
our boat. I had been so busy with the dance school, I hadn't given
much thought to the boat, but I knew it was time for us to begin
Frank's dream.

"I can hardly wait to begin," I said. "I know once you get
started you'll finish our boat."

"Well," Frank replied, "we'd better take some sailing lessons.
I haven't sailed since I was a teenager."

I laughed. "The only boats I've ever been on were the Queen
Mary when I came over from England, and the Cunard Cruise
Line when we took Brock to see his grandfather. They're big
ships. I've never been on anything smaller."

"First, we need a set of plans. I've been looking at a trimaran
designed by Pivar. The model I like is forty feet long and twenty-

two feet wide. It's really a roomy boat with lots of cabin space. A trimaran won't heel over as much as a single hulled boat, so you'll feel more comfortable. This will be a real adventure and we'll learn together," Frank said. "If we give it our best, we'll do just fine."

I loved Frank for his confidence that anything was possible if one has the right attitude and determination.

Frank checked a map to see if there was a harbor close to Sunnyvale. We were surprised to find one only a few miles away in a small town named Alviso at the southern end of San Francisco Bay.

The next Saturday, we drove to Alviso and walked around the harbor. We were surprised to see quite a number of boats being built. We stopped to talk with a man who was working on a trimaran. He was agreeable to showing us the interior. He warned us to be careful climbing the ladder.

He hadn't finished building the boat yet, but I was impressed with the amount of room below deck. "The plans are for sale if you're interested," the man told us. "I may just give up on this. It's too much work."

"We're interested if the price is right," Frank said.

We were only able to afford half the plans, but the man promised to keep the other half until we could pay him for it. We went to the lumber yard and bought $10.00 worth of plywood to begin building our boat. As we loaded the plywood into the car, Frank said, "Terrie, I always seem to be thanking you for your confidence in me. I promise you that once I start our boat, I'll finish it. It'll take a few years, but I plan to retire at fifty-five and then we can sail our dream around the world."

Once we were home, Frank measured the yard. "The boat will be forty feet long and twenty-two feet wide, so it'll take up most of the yard. I've already talked to a crane company and they tell me taking it over the house with a crane will be no problem. We have no wires to avoid and the roof is almost flat."

Our boys helped with some of the work, but they had many other interests taking their time. Brock was in his sophomore year of high school and active in baseball, basketball and football. Kent was in junior high and he kept busy with other activities and small jobs like cutting lawns for neighbors and carrying groceries to people's cars. He was always busy making a few dollars.

"I'm going to save my money so I can go to Europe when I get out of high school," he told us.

We enjoyed Brock's years at Fremont High School. Frank and I never missed a basketball or football game. Neither of us put any pressure on Brock, but he was never satisfied with his game. He always wanted to do better. One of our friends remarked that after the games, the cheerleaders ran around Brock like bees around a honey pot.

Frank relived his youth in Brock. He wanted his boy to be the athlete he never had the chance or natural ability to be.

Kent went to all the games with us. We didn't realize that the attention we gave to his older brother made him determined to succeed at something different. Kent had a lot of drive and determination, plus my spirit of adventure.

By 1965, the trimaran was beginning to take shape. I helped to fiberglass the three hulls and I found myself fascinated watching the resin soak into the cloth and become a hard finish on the plywood. What a long and tedious job. Many areas didn't take well and we had to redo them. Frank was a perfectionist. We bought material for the boat as we could afford it. That way, we never went into debt.

One day, Frank announced that the hulls were ready to be turned over and set in place. He was a long way from completing the boat. The hulls needed to be joined by the crossarms to make them into one unit. The deck, the interior and the pilot house still had to be built, plus we needed to buy and mount the engine. Luckily, I had a cousin in Oregon who was in the steel business and he said he could find an engine for us when the time came.

Frank said, "I'll need about ten fellows to help turn the hulls over. Brock can get a couple of his football buddies and Kent can help, too."

We provided the beer and watched the operation on the following Saturday morning. By following Frank's instruction, the operation went smoothly. Soon the three hulls were settled in the cradles Frank had built for them. The boat looked even bigger now that I could see the full width of the hulls placed properly, right side up. They placed the two smaller hulls on each side of the bigger one in the middle.

The next step was to make the crossarms that would connect the hulls. What a momentous day. Our friends who'd doubted us, now began to believe that Frank would complete his boat. I was very proud of my husband. He was building his dream boat with very little money, the simplest of hand tools, and with hard work and determination, never losing interest and enthusiasm.

In December that year, I surprised Frank. I had ordered the lumber to build the crossarms and it would be delivered to the house. "This is your Christmas present," I told him. "Actually, it's my gift, too."

Frank could not have been happier. May and Pud came from Winnipeg to spend Christmas with us and the boys were delighted to have a real family Christmas. They loved their aunt and uncle who were like grandparents to them. .

Pud was impressed with the Trimaran.

May said, "I can't believe one person could build such a huge boat."

"I get a lot of help from Terrie and the boys," Frank said, "but more important, I've had a great deal of encouragement."

Having May and Pud with us made Christmas wonderful. Frank and I enjoyed every minute of their visit. Pud seemed amazed at how much of the boat Frank had completed. "You always had an imagination, but this is more than that, it's a real accomplishment. I'm real proud of you, Frank."

Brock graduated from high school in 1965. Frank and I watched our son receive his diploma and a special stadium blanket as an award for his athletic accomplishments. Brock had grown into a good looking, 6'4" young man with a charming smile.

Kent graduated from junior high school that year. Shorter than his brother, Kent had broad shoulders, and a wonderful sense of humor. Even at his age, he talked a lot about traveling.

Brock enrolled at Foothill College and was soon selected as a tight-end on the football team. Kent began high school and was a popular member of his freshman class. He never had a problem finding jobs after school and on Saturdays. He continued to save his "traveling" money.

The boys had a weekly allowance for doing chores around the house, plus they earned extra cash doing odd jobs after school. Frank and I felt it was important to teach them to be responsible with their money and never spend more than they could afford. This was probably because Frank and I had never had anyone to back us up if we got into debt.

Frank spent every free minute working on the trimaran. The interior structure was in place and I could see where my galley would be and how the bunks would fit into the hulls. He designed the cabin top and bought Plexiglas for the windows.

I was very involved with recital plans that year. I'd presented "The Wizard of Oz" the previous year and it had been so successful, I decided to try another play. This time, I chose "Peter Pan."

Janie Muirhead, one of my best students with a good personality and abundant energy, was a perfect Peter. One of the six-year-olds played Nana the dog, and a very tiny girl did a beautiful job playing the part of Tinkerbell.

Another apt student danced the role of Wendy. One of my older girls danced the role of Captain Hook. The music was lively and the costumes, perfect.

It had been 12 years since I opened my school. One of my first students was now assisting me. A few days before the Peter Pan recital, she approached me and said, "I'm thinking of starting a school of my own. I don't want to go on to college, so I was wondering if you could you give me some idea how to begin?"

I was quite amazed for I had no idea she had that in mind. Leigh Powell had been in my classes since she was eight years old and now she was a vivacious 19-year-old.

"Well, Leigh, if you're sure that's what you want, I may have a plan for you. I've been considering a change," I said. "Maybe you'd like to take over this school."

"Why give it up?" Leigh said. "You've done so well."

"Sometimes I get a feeling I should try something different,"
I said. "You're a good teacher and your sister, Gay, is doing
well. She'll soon be old enough to help you. I don't want to see
the school close, but if you took over the school, I'd be happy
knowing it is in good hands."

Leigh was ecstatic. "It's a wonderful opportunity. The
school is so well-established, the location is perfect and we even
have a waiting list of prospective students."

Leigh and I settled on an arrangement for her to purchase
the school, but decided not to mention it to anyone until after
the recital.

Frank was surprised when I told him the news. "Well,
honey, you've worked hard and done a great job with the school.
You deserve a rest. It's time to take it easy for a while."

I shook my head. "You don't understand. I want to get a
part-time job. I don't want to stay home. I have too much energy
for that. I just decided to try something different. Maybe I could
get part-time work as a receptionist in a doctor's or dentist's office
now that the boys are old enough to be alone after school. I could
work on Saturdays, too."

"Do what ever makes you happy," Frank said with a smile.

I checked the newspaper and answered an ad for a
receptionist in a doctor's office at a medical center very close
to Cherry Chase. I was nervous as I dressed for the interview.
I'd never worked in an office and knew nothing of the medical
profession, but I figured there was a first time for everything. Dr.
Aubrey Abramson was a young, friendly Jewish internist with
whom I felt at ease. The interview seemed to go well, but I knew
I didn't have the necessary qualifications for the position. I was
surprised when I received a call from the doctor asking if I could

start to work on May 25. I quickly arranged my classes to move to all day Saturdays and Wednesday afternoons, which would be my days off. I planned the recital for June 6. The next few weeks were hectic as I worked hard at both jobs.

Peter Pan was a huge success. When the children gathered on stage for the finale, I walked on stage and stood with them. The audience gave the children a standing ovation. After everyone was seated again, I called Leigh to my side.

"I'm so happy you enjoyed this recital," I said to the audience. "The children worked very hard and I'm very proud of them. Now, I have an announcement. I'm going to retire and Leigh Powell will be the new owner of the dancing school. She is an excellent teacher and your children will be in good hands." I paused and looked at Leigh. "The students love her. Her sister, Gay, will help with the younger pupils. I will also be close by as I'm not leaving the area, but just changing my career. I could not have managed this recital tonight without Leigh's help. I know she'll do a great job and I hope you'll give her your support. I've enjoyed every minute of my thirteen years teaching your children."

One of the young dancers curtseyed and presented me with a bouquet of red roses. My voice broke and tears rolled down my cheeks as I leaned down to kiss thirteen-year-old Gay Powell, probably my most advanced student. My intuition told me I'd made the right move.

As I left the stage, something told me I needed to have other interests and a steady job for the future. At that time I would never have believed that after Leigh married and had a family, Gay would take over the dancing school. She's still running the school very successfully after all these years.

Brock was doing well at De Anza College, but he seemed to be uncertain as to what he wanted to do with his life. He played first string on the football squad and was a popular member of the team.

Even though he had a few girlfriends, he didn't seem to be serious about anyone in particular. The war in Vietnam was causing much concern in the U.S. Frank and I realized Brock was the right age to enlist or be drafted.

In 1965, when Brock was eighteen, he applied for his American citizenship and in June 1965, he told us he was going to enlist in the Air Force. Frank and I were disappointed. We wanted him to go to a four-year college. After we talked about it for several days, we decided the service might be good for Brock. He could return to college after the war was over and it was better than being drafted into the Army. Also, he might decide to make the military his career.

When Brock left for basic training in Texas, I realized our close little family would never be quite the same.

In the same year, Kent was fourteen. He decided to be a camp counselor for the YMCA boys' summer camp. He needed a physical so we had him see Dr. Abramson. After the exam, the doctor told me he was referring Kent to an orthopedist because Kent had the classic symptoms of CMT, short for Charcoal Marie Tooth disease, the names of the three physicians who discovered the rare condition. The disease causes the muscles below the knee and below the elbow to atrophy in time. "It's not life threatening," Doctor Goldberg the orthopedist said, "but it progresses gradually. It could be in remission for years." He said there was no treatment or cure for it. All we could do was to be optimistic and hope that it would not progress quickly.

Frank and I were very distressed to hear that our ambitious, happy son would have to deal with that problem the rest of his life. It seemed so unfair.

Something told me that Kent had his father's great attitude about accepting what life dealt him. In my heart, I knew Kent would not let it stop him from accomplishing his life goals.

Dr. Goldberg was right when he said Kent would eventually have to wear braces below the knees and his hand muscles would deteriorate.

Kent has been wearing braces on his legs for many years. His feet and hands are affected by muscle loss. But, his father was right. The disease has never slowed Kent down. He has traveled all over the world and become a successful businessman and a grandfather.

In 1967, Maude phoned with the sad news that Pud had died of a heart attack while driving the car. May had been badly injured in the accident and was in the hospital.

The news stunned Frank. His brother, Roy, had died two years earlier and his sister, May, had passed away in Vancouver, Canada, in 1964. The family was getting smaller much too fast.

I had become proficient in my job and admired Dr. Abramson a great deal. He was an excellent physician, extremely cautious and conscientious. He had a large practice and my days were long and hectic as I worked alone in the office. I was a Girl Friday.

Meanwhile, Frank spent every spare moment working on the trimaran. He would come in the house looking like a snowman, his face covered with the material from sanding the resin on the hulls. The huge boat was really taking shape, but it was an unending amount of effort. I never heard Frank complain.

He'd tell me how fascinating it was when he completed another step. He enjoyed seeing his big boat progress.

Kent was doing well in high school. He didn't have too much difficulty with his legs, but his ankles were not strong and his feet seemed to be getting deformed. Frank and I had many concerns, but we knew we could do nothing more. Kent had so many plans for future travels using the money he'd been saving for years.

Lydia passed away suddenly in 1968 after a massive heart attack. Everyone was shocked, especially Frank. Lydia had been like a mother to him. Now, only six of the original eleven brothers and sisters were still living. Maude and Dorothy lived in Winnipeg. Ruth was still living in Vancouver. Chancey and Marguerite had moved to California in the Los Angeles area.

A few months after Lydia died, we learned she had left Frank a small inheritance. I suggested using the money for the trimaran, but Frank said, "We should do something exciting with the money. Would you like to go to Europe? Next year will be our twenty-fifth wedding anniversary. Lydia would love to know she'd given us a second honeymoon."

"That's a wonderful idea. We could visit the family and my friends in England."

"Kent will graduate next year in June and if I can arrange my vacation, how about September next year?"

Dr. Abramson told me he'd close the office for those three weeks, and he and I would have our vacations at the same time. What a perfect situation.

We made arrangements for our flight with a charter airline and were told we would be informed when our reservation was confirmed.

Early in 1969, Frank told me he'd been experiencing some problems with his legs. "It's strange. When I climb the ladder to work on the boat, I don't have a problem, but if I walk on flat pavement for a block, I find I have to stop until the cramps go away in my legs."

I arranged an appointment for Frank with Dr. Abramson. I wanted him in tiptop condition for our trip.

Dr. Abramson called us into his office after examining Frank. "I'm pretty sure that you have a circulatory problem in your legs, Frank. The pulses in your groin are almost impossible to detect. I want you to see Dr. Zanger who's a cardiovascular specialist and an expert in his field. He was a student when I was in residency."

After seeing Dr. Zanger, Frank came home with startling news. "I guess it's a trip to the hospital for me. Dr. Zanger wants to do an angiogram to see how much blockage I have in the arteries in my legs. Depending on how severe it is, I may have to have a bypass to correct the problem."

I couldn't believe it. I held on to a chair to steady myself. Frank had never been sick and to find out surgery was necessary really scared me.

"It sounds like a big deal," Frank said, calmly, "but it's really not that bad. Dr. Zanger said I could wait, but I told him about our trip and how I want to be able to walk everywhere in Europe. He'll schedule some tests next week and the bypass surgery as soon as possible."

Frank saw Dr. Zanger the following week who scheduled an angiogram that confirmed his suspicion about Frank having a blockage in the arteries in his legs. A bypass would be necessary.

When I left Frank at the hospital the following Tuesday, it was the first time we'd been apart since my trip to England with Brock in 1947.

The day of the surgery, I took Frank to the hospital before I went to the office. I was very nervous, but I knew he had the best doctors and they would call me as soon as the surgery was over. When I left, I kissed Frank. He gave me a hug and said, "It's just another challenge. You know I'll be okay."

I was glad to be busy at the office that morning. I had a hard time concentrating on my work as I waited for a call from Dr. Zanger. Finally, I picked up the phone and heard the doctor say, "Well, Terrie, the surgery went just like the textbook says it should. Frank is in the recovery room and should be awake and able to see you tonight. I have him in intensive care for a day or two. You should have him home in a week. Now, let me have a word with Dr. Abramson."

I said a big prayer of thanks and relaxed, knowing the worst was over. Frank was quite a guy. He'd told me the operation would be just like one more trip over Germany and he had managed to survive many of those.

After I got my nerves under control, I said a prayer to thank God. I wished the time would go by quickly so I could get to the hospital. After we closed the office, Dr. Abramson asked me to come into his office for a minute.

"Please, may I close the office," I said. "I'd really like to get to the hospital to see Frank."

"First, I need to talk with you, Terrie."

A feeling of dread came over me as I sat down. I knew instinctively something wasn't right. "Please tell me everything is okay."

"I want to explain about two miracles we had today. Frank came through the surgery very well. That is miracle number one. The second one is that by doing the surgery, Dr. Zanger discovered a cancerous lymph node that would never have been detected if Frank had not had the surgery. The node was behind the wall of the stomach. Now that we know about it, we can do something. I would prefer that you not tell Frank, yet. We have to be sure and also give him time to recover from today's ordeal."

I felt myself breaking out in a cold sweat. The word cancer seemed to flash in front of me. I held a tight grip on the chair as waves of dizziness came over me. I was in shock.

"Terrie, you must not assume the worst until Frank sees one of the hematologists. As soon as he's well enough, I'll have Dr. Michaels see him. They're making great strides in the research of blood-type cancers. And, we found it early. Now, you go to the hospital and give Frank a big smile. You must be strong if you're going to help him recover."

Frank was smiling as I walked into the Intensive Care Unit. I leaned down to kiss him, fighting to hold back my tears.

"You see, honey, I told you it would be fine."

I used every bit of strength I had to look happy.

"Do you mind having a husband with Dacron tubing in his legs? Dr. Zanger says I'll be home in a week and then we can start getting ready for that trip to Europe."

Knowing Frank, that was exactly what we'd do. He looked at what life held for him and accepted it. I wished I could look at it the same way.

My heart was heavy as I walked into the house that evening. All of a sudden, I felt so alone. I wanted to find a way to think the doctors were wrong. Everyone makes mistakes, I told myself. Maybe the lymph node was benign and Frank would be fine. This was one situation I could do nothing about. I'd just have to have faith in God and Dr. Michaels.

When Kent came in from work, I made us some tea and gave him the news. Kent said, "Dad's strong. He'll be fine. Doctors can be wrong, too, Mom. When can I go see him?"

"I'll go to the hospital first thing in the morning and then you can see him for a few minutes later in the day."

Kent's attitude made me feel better and although I didn't sleep well, I was able to get some rest that night. When I hurried to the hospital the next morning, Frank looked stronger. They'd be moving him to a room the next day.

"You look tired. Please don't get sick worrying, honey," he told me. "I'll be home and well before you know it."

The mail that day brought more disturbing news. A letter from the charter company said they had overbooked and unless someone cancelled, Frank and I would not have seats on the plane. I felt sick. How could I break the news to Frank? I wrote a letter to the airline telling them the situation and begged them to try to find a place for us.

That evening, when I visited Frank, he was a little more subdued. "Honey, I know now why you looked so pale today. Kent let the cat out of the bag this afternoon. He told me about the cancer thing. I don't quite understand what it's all about, but I don't intend to let it get the best of me."

I was shocked that Kent had told Frank about the cancer. I realized I hadn't told him Dr. Abramson would talk to Frank and we were not to say anything. I knew Kent would feel badly. I decided not to mention it to him. He was troubled about his dad's condition as it was.

Frank said, "Remember, I've got to finish our boat so we can sail around the world. By the way, I've been thinking of names for her while I'm lying here. How do you like the name El Curioso?

It means The Curious."

My husband's positive attitude helped me get through that visit. I decided not to mention the problem with the airline. The only thing I could do was pray the charter airline would give me yet another miracle.

The lymph node biopsy showed Frank had lymposarocoma. His condition was systemic and would have to be treated by chemotherapy. Dr. Michaels gave Frank a physical two weeks after the surgery and started him on a therapy regimen to get his blood count under control. The first thing Frank asked Dr. Michaels was permission to go on the trip to Europe.

I heard from the travel agent and breathed a sigh of relief. They confirmed our reservations. I never told Frank. I'm so glad I kept that secret.

Brock was stationed in Alaska in 1969. He'd joined the Air Force basketball team and also played softball for his unit. He'd be coming home on leave before we left for Europe. I hadn't told him his dad had cancer. I felt it would be easier to explain when he came home.

Kent graduated from high school in June 1969. Frank and I watched the ceremony with pride as our young son accepted his diploma. Kent appeared very sure of himself as he walked up to the podium. He'd saved enough money for his trip to Europe and would be leaving in two days. He and three friends planned to backpack throughout Europe for three months. Frank and I would start our trip only two days after Kent was scheduled to return.

As I helped Kent with his backpack, I wondered how he would manage with very little money, but I didn't worry because he seemed so confident and I wanted him to be able to do what he'd planned. I hoped his feet and legs would not be a problem. His attitude was so good, I found it hard to be concerned. I gave Kent a hug and he promised to write.

Frank drove the boys to the Oakland airport and when he returned he told me, "You know, this is the best education Kent will ever have. He'll learn to be self-sufficient."

"I hope he'll settle down, eventually. I'd like to see both the boys get their college degrees one day," I said.

Kent had a wonderful time as he toured Europe. He would be in England visiting my sister Kathleen when his cousin, Richard, got married. Kathleen loaned him a borrowed suit so he could attend the wedding. He made quite an impression on the family.

Kent really enjoyed meeting everyone in my family and they were interested in all of his travels.

Richard and his new wife, Katie, were planning to come to California for a "working" honeymoon. They hoped to find jobs and earn some money to help with their trip. Frank and I offered our home to the newlyweds.

The summer was hectic. Katie and Richard stayed with us for almost three months. They were disappointed because Richard couldn't find work. Kate did manage to get a job as a waitress. They counted her tips each night, trying to save every extra penny they could. We gave them the use of a car so they could do some sightseeing.

A much more mature Brock came home on leave for two of those weeks. Life in our small house was stressful. Even though Frank tolerated his chemotherapy well, the little black cloud still hung around. I tried hard to keep the fear of cancer from my mind.

Brock was distressed when we told him about his father's condition, but once again, Frank's positive attitude seemed to assure everyone that he could overcome his illness. Brock was assigned to a base in Fairbanks, Alaska for six more months before coming home for Christmas.

Kent returned home from Europe looking happy. He and his friends, Lance, Frank and Eric came home with wonderful stories of their adventures in Europe. Those boys had been friends all through school and are still good friends, except for Eric who died a few years after their trip.

As I listened to my young son, I realized Frank was right. Kent had learned a great deal about people in other countries and could appreciate the opportunities for freedom offered in America.

When Frank and I left for Europe in September, Kent promised to take care of the house and register for junior college. I was confident that Frank would be fine for our vacation. He had no problems with his medication and Dr. Michael was very pleased with his response to the chemotherapy.

Our plane landed in Frankfurt, Germany. There, we purchased a Eurorail pass and began a wonderful journey through Germany, Italy, Holland, France, Austria and finally England.

We both felt just like newlyweds, holding hands and stopping every once in a while to have a hug or kiss, as if everything was perfect. The little black cloud had vanished.

We walked and admired everything we'd heard about in books—the Trevi Fountain, the Vatican, the Coliseum and all the beautiful cathedrals and churches.

We took a train ride through Austria. The scenery there was particularly breathtaking. We found the ancient history fascinating. The cobblestone streets and the charming old buildings took us back in time. We were happy to be able to enjoy everything together.

"We'll come back," Frank said. "We'll have to live forever to see more of this world." After a short pause, he added, "And we'll do a lot of sailing in the Caribbean and other places."

"Of course we will," I said, "when the boat is finished."

I said a silent prayer asking God to give Frank time so we could come back to see more of Europe together and to complete our boat.

Billy and Marjorie met us at the station in Nottingham. They looked older, but after all, it had been 19 years since my last visit to England. As we drove to Sherwood, I could see many changes in Nottingham, although Victoria Station was still the same. I felt a twinge of nostalgia as I looked across the street at the YMCA. So much had happened since I'd met Frank there in 1941.

Kathleen and Phil were happy to see us. They told us how much they'd enjoyed seeing Kent. When we were alone, Marjorie asked me about Frank. I told her exactly what the problem was and how we'd been fortunate to discover it early. "He's the bravest man I've ever known," Marjorie said. "His attitude makes all of us feel confident he'll conquer this terrible thing."

"I hope they'll come up with something soon. Dr. Michaels tells us they're doing a lot of research for Hodgkin's disease and leukemia. I try to be as optimistic as Frank," I said.

When the time came for us to return to California, I felt almost relieved. I was anxious to see Kent, but also I wanted Frank to see Dr. Michaels and have his blood count checked. Both of us hoped that somewhere Lydia would know how grateful we were for the unforgettable trip that had meant so much to us.

The flight home was uneventful. Kent was at the airport to meet our plane, happy and smiling. "Now, we can compare notes," Kent said. "I doubt that we stayed in the same places, but I'm sure we saw many of the same sights."

"We have a lot to talk about, son," Frank said. "Now, I plan to get on with our trimaran. I want to do some off-shore sailing for our next vacation."

Christmas 1969 was a memorable one for the Dagg family. Brock was home on a two week leave. Frank's sister, Dorothy, and brother-in-law, Charlie, came from Winnipeg for the holidays. We invited his sister, Marguerite, and her husband, Don, who were now living in Ojai, California, as well as Frank's brother, Chauncy, and his wife, Madeline, from San Jose. To have so many family members with us to celebrate Christmas meant a lot to me.

When we were all seated around the table, Frank proposed a toast. "This is the first time we've been together for Christmas since the children were small. Now, as we get older, our family is getting smaller, and we must all make an effort to be together more often." Lydia, May, Ruth, Pud and Roy were already gone.

Everyone agreed. As they left, however, I felt a chill around my heart. I wondered if that would be the last time.

As we said goodbye to Dorothy and Charlie, I felt especially sad. Dorothy was my favorite sister-in-law. I would always remember the times in England when Charlie had been so supportive during the problems with my family. I wished they lived closer. Winnipeg seemed so far away from California.

After the holiday, Kent decided to move into an apartment with two of his friends. He was doing well in college and working part-time at a Toys 'R' Us store. He never seemed to have a problem getting a job and he always saved his money.

In 1970, Frank and I were living alone again. The house seemed quiet. We were so used to the boys and their friends running in and out at all hours.

I decided to make one of the bedrooms into a den. We moved a couple of chairs and the TV in there. The room became quite cozy. Our house was small, but the builder had laid it out quite well. Frank was handy with tools, and we had added a half-bath, plus extra shelving in the closet. We were both happy we had been able to afford this house as it proved to be a good investment.

Frank never tired of working on the boat. I kept busy with the house, my work with Dr. Abramson, and helping Frank with the trimaran on the weekends. We had never-ending sanding to do, but the big boat was really taking shape.

Brock was on leave for three weeks that Christmas. A friend of his had introduced him to Karen. She was a very attractive young woman. They spent every day together and Brock seemed to enjoy being with her. He'd been concerned with his dad's condition to the point where we were glad to see him having some fun on his leave.

One Sunday in February, we had a visit from Karen. "Brock is going to be calling from Virginia around three o'clock," she said.

When the phone rang, Frank said, "That must be Brock. Why don't you answer it, Karen?"

We heard her say, excitedly, "Yes, whenever you say."

I knew Brock had asked her to marry him.

Frank went to the phone. "Well, son, you're certainly full of surprises. This is unexpected, but if you're sure, we welcome Karen to our family."

We both gave Karen a hug. Then, Frank said to Karen, "You and Brock have known each other for such a short time, but if you're sure you love one another, we could not be happier." Still, we were apprehensive.

They set the date for April 25th. The next few weeks were hectic. Karen's parents planned a formal wedding. Brock asked Kent to be his best man and Karen's two younger brothers, Chris and Eric, would be the ushers.

I went with Karen and her mother to select her wedding gown. During the outing, I was shocked at the way her mother behaved. It was obvious she had no regard for Karen's father. I realized that Karen had been raised differently from the way we raised Brock. There seemed to be no love in their family.

I felt very uncomfortable. When I mentioned my feelings to Frank, he agreed that the family seemed cold.

At a bridal shower, I was embarrassed by some of the remarks the bride's mother made in front of my friends. Oh, well, I told myself. It'll be okay. Karen isn't her mother.

Frank and I remained concerned that Brock and Karen had known each other for too short a time. However, with Frank's condition first on my mind, I didn't want more problems. We went along with the wedding plans and hoped for the best.

Frank was tiring more often, now. I tried to persuade him to work less on the boat, but he seemed determined to keep busy. He still went to work at Hewlett-Packard and on the weekends he spent his days sanding the hulls for hours until he was satisfied they were smooth enough.

April 25, 1970, was a beautiful spring day. I sat with Frank in the church filled with many good friends as I looked at Brock and Kent standing together in front of the altar. I was a proud mom.

Brock was handsome. Kent had an infectious smile. Thoughts raced through my mind. I remembered my wedding when I'd been surrounded by strangers. I thanked God that Frank had lived to see his sons grow up. Both boys loved and respected their father and he knew this. As I turned to my husband, I could see by his expression that he was as proud as I was.

Karen was a beautiful bride. When Brock and Karen took their vows and turned to walk down the aisle, their faces were radiant. Frank and I greeted many of the friends we'd made in California. Our only regret was the absence of our families. We wished Karen's family had been warmer, but they weren't.

The young couple went to Lake Tahoe for a short honeymoon before Brock had to return to Virginia. After Brock and his bride left, things once again were back to our normal routine.

My cousin in Oregon, Bill Wild, had acquired a used engine made by Gray Marine for the trimaran and had shipped it to us. Frank was working on the interior of the big boat. I tried to persuade him to relax as he looked worn out. I was happy when he suggested a vacation.

"I'd like to go to Winnipeg," he said. "How do you feel about driving up there? We could go along the Trans-Canada Highway. This time we can enjoy different kinds of scenery. I think it'd be relaxing. You know how I love to drive."

I agreed, but I was a little apprehensive as Frank was losing more weight and was obviously tiring more easily. I worried that the long drive would be too much and I knew he would not let me take over. I also knew he wanted to see his family. We would just have to take our time and stop when he was tired. We decided to go in June. I arranged for time off. Dr. Abramson agreed that a trip to Winnipeg would be good for Frank. Dr. Michaels felt Frank's condition was stable, so we planned the trip for the second week in June, 1970.

We were amazed at the changes that had taken place in Winnipeg since we'd left. The city had grown. We went directly to Dorothy and Charlie's home where we'd been invited to stay. They greeted us warmly, and after a light meal, we drove over to see Pud's wife, May.

After Pud's death, May had sold the little house in Norwood and now lived in an apartment. Frank and I were shocked to see the change in the active woman we remembered. May walked with a cane and seemed so much older. She broke down when she looked at Frank.

"You look so much like my Pud," she said. "I miss him so terribly. Seeing you both is wonderful"

The whole family was at Maude's for dinner the following evening. The big house seemed empty without Bob who had died many years before. Maude looked as vibrant as ever — still a handsome woman, running her florist shop with great success. She'd become an Alderwoman on the Winnipeg City Council and was well-liked by everyone.

We visited friends and went to see the little house we'd lived in on Breamar Avenue. Some of our neighbors still lived there. When we drove out to Charleswood, we were amazed at the development that had taken place over the years. The area, that had been so barren and isolated when we bought our first house, was now a lovely community with colorful landscaping and new schools. We were happy to see our old house had been well cared for.

When it came time to go home, I found it hard to control my

emotions. I knew Frank would not return to his birthplace, but we took wonderful memories back with us and left everyone in the family feeling confident that Frank would be fine. He looked and acted as if his health was perfect.

Frank drove out of the city and headed toward Montana. We'd decided we could make Montana the first night, but we hadn't counted on severe weather conditions. Rain pelted us so hard, Frank suggested stopping at a small town near the Montana border. We couldn't find a decent place to stay so we decided to try the next town. Suddenly, we hit a flooded area and the car hydroplaned.

Frank cried, "Hang on."

I felt the car go backwards and then we turned over. When the car righted, we were embedded in a deep ditch filed with mud.

The car faced the opposite direction and our luggage had flown out the rear window into the ditch. Frank's knee had pushed the emergency flasher on the steering wheel and I could see a little red light going on and off as I sat, my body rigid.

I heard Frank say, "Are you all right, Terrie?"

I thought if I relaxed, all the bones in my body would break. Soon I discovered I wasn't hurt at all. The only injury I had was a tiny scratch where my leg hit the dashboard.

"How about you, Frank?"

"No problems, honey. Now, I hope you'll believe me when I tell you when it's time, it's time. Nothing changes that. This just wasn't our time."

I have always remembered Frank saying that.

A patrolman spotted the flasher and stopped at the top of the ditch. Frank yelled that nobody was hurt, so there was no need

for an ambulance. The patrolman called for a wrecking truck.
They pried open the doors so Frank and I could crawl through.
Then they took the wheels off the car in order to pull it out of the
ditch.

Before leaving Winnipeg, Maude had given us a beautiful
china pitcher and washbasin, and a small antique bedroom chair.
Luckily, we had wrapped the china in a blanket and the chair
in some cardboard before we'd put them in the trunk of the car.
Our luggage was on the back seat. When the car righted, we saw
everything had been thrown out of the trunk into the muddy
ditch. Miraculously, nothing seemed to have broken.

We were dirty and knew we'd be stiff the next day. When
the policeman told us there'd been three fatal accidents on the
same stretch of road that night, I realized how fortunate we were.
I also knew that Frank was right. It hadn't been our time to die.

The policeman took us and our luggage to a motel. We
asked the policeman if we could store the chair and china at the
police station overnight. After a hot shower, we fell into bed and
tried to sleep. We were exhausted. Frank pointed out that the
motel was really not much better than the one we'd passed up
before the accident.

In the morning, we looked outside. Frank spotted a milk
truck. We asked the driver if he would give us a ride into
Glendive, the little town where the car had been taken. After a
light breakfast, we went to the garage. When we looked at our
badly damaged car, we couldn't believe we'd walked away with
nothing but a scratch.

Frank said, calmly, "Well, since the airlines are on strike,
I guess we'll have to rent a car. We certainly can't get Maude's
gifts home any other way. You once told me you loved my spirit

of adventure. I hope you still feel that way. There's never a dull moment with the Daggs."

"Renting a car is a good idea," I said. "We'll have to call George and Lu to tell them what happened. We can visit them some other time."

George and Lu Muirhead lived in Renton, outside of Seattle. We'd planned to visit them for several days on our drive down the Washington and Oregon coast to California.

"Why call them?" Frank said. "We'll tell them ourselves. Since we'll have a car, we can stop in Renton just like we planned. I bet they'll get a kick out of our adventure."

And that's what we did, only we made our visit just an overnight. We felt rested and ready to journey on after spending time with our dear friends.

I can't keep from smiling as I remember Frank's wonderful attitude. Nothing ever seemed to faze him. After almost being killed in the car accident, he was acting as if nothing had happened.

I felt a twinge of anxiety when I remembered that the biggest adventure of his life might never happen. I said a silent prayer to God asking Him to spare my husband long enough to complete his dream and sail our trimaran.

A smiling Kent was waiting for us at the house. "You sure know how to shake a guy up. I'm certainly glad to see you both. You look like a couple of weary travelers, but you're safely home and that's all that matters."

We bought a car the following day and life returned to normal for a few months. Brock and Karen would be home for Christmas and I was happy as I once again baked, cleaned and planned for a family Christmas.

During that Christmas in 1970, Brock took me outside to talk with me. "Dad has lost more weight. He doesn't seem to be as strong. Is the medicine still working? Mom, promise to let me know if you need me. Please don't try to carry the whole burden."

By October 1971, Frank was having problems with abdominal pains. After an X-ray, Dr. Michaels told me a tumor was causing a blockage in his urethra. "Frank will need surgery to clear the blockage."

With his usual good attitude, Frank laughed. "Well, I guess we could have called Rotorooter to get my plumbing unclogged."

Frank tolerated the surgery well, and we began to plan for Christmas 1971. Brock and Karen were stationed at Hamilton Air Force Base in Marin County. They would have Christmas Eve with her family, then dinner with us on Christmas Day. Kent was working part time at Toys 'R' Us and going to college. He'd be home for the holiday, also. Christmas would be a happy time despite our concerns.

This holiday turned out to be our last Christmas together as a family. It became apparent that the chemotherapy was not effective and Frank began to lose more weight and experience more abdominal pain. Dr. Michaels told us the radiation treatments were the only other method to relieve the pain. I knew this was a last resort because radiation supposedly spread the type of cancer Frank had been diagnosed with originally.

Frank sensed how worried I was. He'd tell me, "Don't worry, honey. I plan to see the year 2000."

I wished so often that I had his positive attitude. He always seemed to be lifting my spirits instead of the other way around.

Frank was disturbed because he knew the trimaran was

being neglected, but he didn't have the strength to climb the ladder to work on the big boat anymore.

Each morning I drove Frank to the hospital radiation department. The first treatment worked wonders. Frank felt much better and was able to walk to the car without help. However, he soon was unable to go to work at Hewlett-Packard, and he slept a lot of the time. I tried to keep a good attitude, but every day I'd see Frank become weaker.

One day, Frank took my hand and said, "Terrie, we've been very lucky. We've been together for twenty-seven years and I wouldn't have changed a day. I fell in love with you the first time I saw you at the Y, and when we walked to your house in Nottingham, I knew I wanted to spend my life with you. You have been a wonderful wife, never losing faith in me. And we've two great sons. My only regret is I haven't finished our dream. I'm not afraid of dying, honey, but I worry that you'll not be able to cope."

I put my arms around him. "Frank, I can't imagine my life without you. We've been through so much together. If I had my life to live over, I wouldn't change a thing."

A few days later, I heard a tap on the front door. I opened it to find Maude standing there. I was shocked to see Frank's oldest sister at our door at eleven in the morning. She hadn't let us know she was planning to visit. When I recovered from the surprise, I welcomed her with a big hug. I was delighted she had come.

"Maude, I'm so happy to see you. How did you get here? It's such a long journey from Winnipeg."

"Well," she said, "I took a night flight from Winnipeg, a bus from San Francisco Airport to Sunnyvale and a taxi from the bus station. Now I want to see Frank."

I was amazed, but I knew this strong-willed woman would do what she had to. After I took Maude's coat and made coffee, I went to the bedroom to tell Frank she was here.

"Frank, I have a surprise. Guess who's here to see us?"

Frank said, "I know. Maude's here. I heard her come in. I don't want her to see me like this."

I was taken aback by his reaction. "Frank, she's come so far that you can't disappoint her."

Maude was still enjoying her coffee when I went into the kitchen. "Frank doesn't want you to see him. He thinks it will be hard for you since he's very weak and quite thin, now. I think he'll change his mind if we give him some time."

In about a half hour, I witnessed a miracle. Frank walked into the living room, straight and tall, with a grin from ear to ear. "Hello, Maude. Sorry I took so long, but I was slow getting dressed today."

They visited for a while and then Frank said, "Why don't we get in the car. I'd like to take you to see some of the area."

Once again, I was stunned. Frank had not driven the car for weeks and he was talking and laughing like his old self. We even stopped for ice cream cones.

After an early dinner, Frank excused himself. I went with him to the bedroom where he collapsed on the bed. I helped him out of his clothes and into bed. I knew he must be beyond total exhaustion. I couldn't imagine the strength and courage he found that day.

"Well, honey," Frank said. "I do hope Maude will go back to Winnipeg knowing I'm not as sick as she thought. I don't want the family worrying. The family is getting smaller too quickly and they're so far away."

Maude said goodbye to her younger brother the next morning and as I drove her to the San Francisco Airport to catch her plane, Maude became quite emotional.

"Frank made such a huge effort to show me not to worry," Maude said. "He was pushed from pillar to post growing up with just his brothers and sisters to guide him after Mom and Dad died. Maybe that's why he's always been so independent and willing to try anything." Maude stared out the window in silence for quite awhile, and then she said, "You know, he never gave us a moment of concern, Terrie. And we've always been very proud of his war effort."

I could tell from her voice that Maude was holding back her tears. As we approached the airport, she said, "Life seems unfair that he should die so young."

Two days after Maude left, I arranged with the Red Cross to allow Brock to spend some time at home to help his father. When I went to work, Brock would take Frank for his radiation treatments.

One night, Frank was really restless. Brock and I stayed up most of the night. As we sat in the kitchen, Brock told me that he and Karen were having problems. "I wanted a marriage like you and Dad have. Kent and I had such a happy childhood. Our home was always so full of love. Karen and I don't seem to agree on anything and I hate to be always fighting with her."

I looked at my son. "Marriage is not easy," I said. "You have to climb the hills together. Nothing is perfect, but if both partners work at it, marriage can be wonderfully rewarding."

I really thought I was giving Brock good advice, but the years following our talk proved me to be wrong. I've regretted my words many times. Remembering the type of people Karen's family were, I should have known things wouldn't work between Brock and Karen. Her family had different values and ideals, and the kids hadn't dated each other long enough before they married.

Brock went back to his base and I promised to call him at once if his dad got worse.

It was a wonderful relief when Frank's sister Dorothy called from Winnipeg to tell me she would like to spend a few days with me. The effort Frank took when Maude visited had taken its toll. He seemed to be in more pain and he'd lost more weight. I was working in the afternoons and it took most of the morning to get Frank to the hospital and then comfortably settled before I went to the office. When Dorothy arrived, she would be able to take over and be with Frank in the afternoon.

Dr. Michaels had suggested it might be easier if Frank was admitted to the hospital, but I had promised Frank I wouldn't allow that as long as I was able to take care of him.

When Dorothy arrived in San Francisco on April 10, I hurried home from the office. Frank looked better than he had for days, and the three of us enjoyed dinner and a pleasant evening.

Frank finally gave in to exhaustion. He kissed his sister before he went to bed.

"I can't tell you how much it means to have you here, Dorothy. You're like a breath of fresh air. I'm so grateful to you for coming." To know she'd be with Frank while I was at work and that she would call me if necessary was a huge relief. Frank would have things to talk about with his favorite sister. Everything would be so much easier.

Dorothy and I sat up until the early morning hours talking about the family. Dorothy and Charlie had a little granddaughter, Christine. I admired the pictures Dorothy showed me.

"Charlie and I are planning a trip to Europe," Dorothy said. "You know, I've wanted to go there for years and I could never persuade Charlie to take me. But he finally agreed. We have reservations for September and I'm so excited."

The next few days were pleasant. I knew Frank and Dorothy enjoyed a few hours each day chatting and reminiscing.

I'd become acquainted with many of the patients in my years working with Dr. Abramson. One patient was a friendly man named Herb Dorfman, an enthusiastic sailor. He'd show me pictures of his sailboat when he came in for his yearly physical. I knew I'd need advice on how to sell the trimaran when that time arrived. I told Mr. Dorfman about the trimaran one day as he was waiting for the doctor.

I explained that Frank was terminally ill and I'd need to sell our unfinished boat. I asked him if he could give me some advice on how to go about it. I knew I couldn't keep the boat in the backyard when I was alone.

Mr. Dorfman agreed to take a look at the boat. I gave him my address and directions to the house. He was willing to come after work.

I told Dorothy I would watch for Mr. Dorfman and take him directly to the backyard as it was important that Frank not see or hear him from the bedroom. I certainly didn't want Frank to have any idea I was considering selling our boat.

When Mr. Dorfman arrived, I introduced him to Dorothy. We walked around the side of the house to look at the boat.

Mr. Dorfman was impressed with the design. "It's hard to believe this is the work of one man," he said. "It's a beautiful design, built sturdy, and the interior layout is well-planned with plenty of storage space. The workmanship is exceptional," he told me after examining the boat. "I see you also have an engine. Unfortunately, you'll never get what the boat is worth as the labor won't be considered in the price."

"I know," I said.

"The biggest expense is still to come. The rigging and sails are very expensive, Terrie. You should advertise in the San Francisco Chronicle as well as the San Jose Mercury. I'll put an ad in the Lockheed Star for you and a notice at the Oakland Yacht Club in Alameda. That's where I keep my boat."

I was so relieved. Thank goodness I'd contacted him. I thanked Mr. Dorfman and as he left, he told me to be sure to let him know if there was anything more he could do.

Dorothy told me I should stay in touch with him. "He's such a kind and sincere man. He'd be a good friend."

As I got ready to leave for the office after lunch on April 18, I felt uneasy. Dorothy came in from shopping. I mentioned to her that Frank refused to take his pain medicine. "Frank hasn't been very responsive this morning. He seems to be sleeping heavier than usual. Please call me if you think there's any change. I'm only minutes away." I went into the bedroom and kissed Frank. He looked at me intently, then sighed and went back to sleep without a word.

At three o'clock when I answered the phone at the office, I knew it was Dorothy. "Terrie, please come home. Frank's breathing is very shallow.

When I told Dr. Abramson, he said, "Tell the next patient we have an emergency and make an appointment for her on another day. Then call the exchange and tell them to pick up our phone until we get back. I'll take you home."

As Dr. Abramson and I entered Frank's bedroom, the doctor

patted Frank on the shoulder. I was surprised to see Frank open his eyes and say, "Oh, hi doctor."

After examining Frank, Dr. Abramson told me Frank could be in this condition for days. "However, I think it would be a good idea to have the boys come home."

Dorothy promised she'd stay close to Frank. "I'll call if there's any change. You'll be home in about an hour. Please don't worry."

I went to Frank, gave him a kiss and told him I loved him. He looked up at me and said, "Me, too."

I was able to reach both boys by phone. Kent worked in Redwood City, about 12 miles away. Brock and Karen lived in Novato. They would take at least two hours to get to the house bucking the commute traffic. Both boys said they'd come at once.

I had to make a decision about returning to work. I was torn because there was nobody to take over in the one-girl office. Dorothy assured me she'd stay right by Frank and call me immediately if anything changed. I decided to go back to work. I truly believed Frank would be alright.

That day, I made a decision I will always regret.

A half hour later, Kent called. "Mom, please come home. I want you to be with me."

I ran to the doctor. "I have to leave at once."

"I'll take you. Sign us out right now."

When we arrived, I knew I was too late.

Dr. Abramson took me in his arms. "I'm sorry, Terrie. We were just a few minutes too late."

My whole body felt numb.

"I'm surprised Frank left us so soon. When I saw him earlier, I was sure he had more time," Dr. Abramson said. "He's at peace now, Terrie. No more pain."

Kent ran and hugged me. "Oh, Mom, I held Dad's hand and told him how much I loved him. He looked up at me, gave a big sigh and just went to sleep. He was very peaceful."

Karen and Brock arrived too late, also. Brock was frustrated and Karen was crying. "We tried so hard to get here in time. Now I can't say goodbye to Dad," Brock said.

I put my arms around Brock and said, "Dad knows you were here for him. He was so proud of you and Kent. Always remember that. I should have been with him. I'll always regret that I was too late."

"You mustn't feel guilty, dear," Dorothy said. "Frank's biggest concern was leaving you. I believe he waited until you left before he let himself go."

Even at the end, Frank had protected me. All through his illness he always worried if I could be able to cope without him. Now I would not let him down. I would carry on.

I went into the bedroom, closed the door and sat on the bed next to Frank. He looked so young as I held him in my arms. I never wanted to let go. This man had flown 35 missions over Germany without a scratch at the height of World War II; we'd had a terrible accident without getting killed; we'd struggled hard to make a good life for our sons. He was cheated to die at such a young age, not given a chance to fulfill his dream. Then, I remembered him telling me, "When it's time, it's time."

Finally, Dr. Abramson came in and told me I must let Frank go. He had made arrangements with the funeral home.

Frank and I had talked about funerals and we both decided we didn't want a service. We both wanted to be cremated and the ashes scattered over the San Francisco Bay.

For the next few days I was not alone. Neighbors and friends came at all hours.

Dorothy planned to return home on Saturday. On Thursday she said to me, "Terrie, I have a favor to ask of you. The family has a plot in a cemetery in Winnipeg. Would you consider or be willing for me to take Frank's ashes back to Winnipeg?" She said it would mean a lot to the family. "Pud is buried there. We'll have a committal service for the family and Frank's Winnipeg friends."

I readily agreed. Dorothy could take Frank's ashes home to Winnipeg. I didn't think I was going against his wishes to let the family pay their respects and say their goodbyes in their own way.

I asked if I should go with her. "I'll arrange for the time off."

"Really, Terrie, you should stay here. The boys need you. I know how you and Frank felt about funerals. The family will have a committal, not a formal funeral. Maybe you will come for a visit later when things settle down."

I told Dorothy I'd like to arrange for a small marker with Frank's name on it to be placed where they buried his ashes. She agreed and I gave her a check. I felt I was shirking my responsibilities. Dorothy convinced me I was doing the right thing and the family would be grateful. I have never regretted my decision.

Dorothy's love and support helped me get through the worst days of my life. She was wise and understanding. I hated to see her leave. Before she left, she said, "Terrie, that back fence could really stand a coat of paint. It's looking a little rejected."

I knew she was trying to tell me to keep busy so the loneliness wouldn't be so hard.

The house seemed cold and lonely in spite of the warm April day. I went outside and looked at our boat. I climbed the ladder onto the trimaran. As I sat in the cockpit, my tears finally came, and with the tears, relief. Suddenly, I felt Frank was with me. "Our dream will be finished, Frank," I said. "I promise you that one day she'll be sailing on San Francisco Bay."

I lay awake that night, my head filled with questions. Why did this happen? Why Frank? I even had moments when I was angry with Frank for leaving me. At the same time, I was thankful to have my job to keep me busy.

Life was empty without Frank.

Chapter 10

More people answered the advertisements for the trimaran than I'd expected. One young man came out the next week. He offered to buy the boat, but he told me he didn't have the cash. He asked if he could make a small down payment and pay the rest in monthly payments.

I called Herb Dorfman. He cautioned me not to sell unless I was paid in full. "You should sell to someone who doesn't need to make monthly payments and get a bill of sale stating that the boat is no longer your property. That way, you'll protect yourself."

A few days later, a couple in their early twenties came to see the trimaran. After looking it over, George and Jean Barnes made an offer on the boat.

"We want to do some sailing while we're young. We can get a year's leave of absence and if things go well, we may just quit and travel for a few years. We can always get jobs later."

I was impressed by their enthusiasm. I knew they would finish building our trimaran. They agreed to my asking price and the deal was settled. They gave me a check and signed the papers.

"Wow, now we own a boat," they said.

They almost jumped up and down with excitement. When they'd gotten over their delight at finally owning their "dream boat," I explained how Frank had intended to get the boat to the closest harbor.

He planned to hire the Bigge Crane Company that would lift the boat over the house with a crane, put it onto a flatbed truck and transport the trimaran to the harbor in Alviso, the town where Frank and I had first bought the plans nine years before. The Barnes decided to follow Frank's plan.

"It'll take time to arrange for a crane," I told them. "But, if you're anxious to get working on the boat, you're welcome to do so in the backyard."

Dorothy wrote telling me that the family had held a committal service for Frank, performed at the graveside by an Air Force Padre. Some of Frank's old school friends had attended. To me, the committal service was not meaningful. I felt Frank was gone when he closed his eyes for the last time, but I knew it was comforting for the family.

Brock and Karen visited in April with exciting news. Karen was expecting a baby. If the doctor was right, my first grandchild would be born in October. Frank's place on earth would be taken by a new member of the family. I didn't know then that Grant would be born on October 12, his grandfather Frank's birthday.

I kept busy sewing and knitting, filling the lonely evening hours thinking about the baby. It didn't take long to realize I'd made a mistake when I told George and Jean they could work on the boat in the backyard. When I came home in the evenings and heard the familiar sounds of sanding and hammering, I could hardly stand it. My emotions became unbearable as I looked outside, expecting to see Frank working there.

George and Jean realized how uncomfortable I was, so they arranged for a larger crane than was really necessary, but was available immediately. In early June, George told me he'd made arrangements to take the trimaran to Alviso and work on it at the boatyard there.

The operation went as smoothly as Frank had predicted. The crane operator put the big boom over the house and picked the boat up as if it were a toy. He set the boat down on a flatbed truck on the street, where it stayed overnight.

I had offered George and Jean my guest room, but they said, "Thanks, but we have our camper truck and we want to be near the boat. We'll park out front, if that's all right with you."

I slept fitfully and was up at dawn to find the young couple already awake. They joined me for breakfast at 5:00 a.m. That early, when the streets were free of traffic, two motorcycle policemen arrived to escort the trimaran to its new home. I was very surprised to see Dr. and Emily Abramson drive up. A few neighbors were also waiting on the sidewalk.

I could hardly see through my tears as I watched the parade move down Susan Way and out of sight. I walked into the backyard and looked at the emptiness. I got a hammer and dismantled the big cradles that had held the trimaran for nine years. As soon as the stores opened, I grabbed my purse and headed for Home Depot where I bought bags of soil and grass seed, and spent the day leveling the ground and planting a lawn. That night, I fell into bed completely exhausted. I'd managed to get through one of the most difficult days of my life. If only Frank could have seen that amazing dream of his on its way to the water.

The Barnes promised to keep in touch with me and to let me know how the work on the boat was going. I knew Frank's labor would not be wasted.

The summer of 1972 was lonely, even though Brock and Karen visited often and I had many wonderful friends. I had missed my friend Shirley and was elated when Howard was transferred back to California from Connecticut. Shirley and Howard now lived in Saratoga. I kept busy with my job and the house, but nothing seemed to fill the void left by Frank's death.

In June, Kent told me he was taking another trip. This time he was going to the South Seas as crew on a large sailing ship. Toys R Us gave him leave to go with the promise his job would be waiting when he returned. It was hard for me to see him leave. My youngest son was restless and unable to settle down. Kent celebrated his 21st birthday in Bora Bora.

When he returned, he wanted to leave the Bay Area. He enrolled at Shasta College in Redding, about 280 miles north of Sunnyvale, got a job and met a girl named Sharon Partain. Kent called to tell me how much he liked Sharon's family. I also received a letter from Sharon saying she liked Kent and would wait for him to settle down.

Herb Dorfman called me in August and asked me out for dinner. I refused. I was not ready yet. I had kept Frank's letters and other memoirs, and they were a comfort to me. I spent the evenings re-reading what Frank had written to me when I was in England before we married.

In September, I got a call from Charlie. He told me Dorothy wasn't well. She'd been suffering from back pain. X-rays showed she had a malignant and inoperable tumor on her spine. They canceled their trip to Europe. I was heartbroken. My sister-in-law was such a giving person. It seemed so unfair she'd been dealt such a cruel blow. I hoped the medication would help, but I knew that would be a temporary delay on the inevitable.Everything went well with Karen's pregnancy. My first grandson, Allen Grant Dagg, was born on Frank's birthday, October 12, 1972.

Grant was a beautiful baby. Brock and Karen were so happy to have a son. Brock said, "I hope our son will inherit his grandfather's disposition since he was born on Dad's birthday."

I hoped the same thing.

I decided I must do my best to make Christmas 1972 a happy time. I bought and decorated a small tree and arranged gifts under it for everyone. I got a little red wagon for Grant, even though he was only two months old.

Brock and Karen said they would spend Christmas Eve with me, but they would be with Karen's folks for Christmas dinner. I was not included.

Kent had asked if I would mind him spending Christmas with Sharon's family in Redding. I told him I was fine with that. I knew the boys would miss their dad on the first holiday without him.

I was excited on Christmas Eve as I waited for Brock and Karen to arrive with my grandson. When I greeted them at the door, Grant wasn't with them.

"I didn't want to disturb Grant," Karen said. "He was asleep when we left."

Having my grandson on his first Christmas would have been such a comfort to me. Instead, disappointment filled my heart to overflowing.

We opened gifts and had a nice evening even though things seemed to be a little strained. Brock didn't seem to be happy. I didn't sleep well that night.

I got through Christmas Day by dropping in on my friends, Gloria and Ed, and Shirley and Howard. I refused dinner as my emotions were too close to the surface when I was around families.

I was happy when the holiday was over and I was back at work. Early in January, Herb Dorfman called the office for an appointment. Before he left the office, he asked how things were going and again offered to take me to dinner the following Saturday. This time I accepted his offer. I called Shirley for help in picking out an outfit. "I'm so nervous," I told her.

It seemed strange to be going out with a man after 27 years of marriage. When the phone rang, I wondered if Herb had changed his mind. Charlie was on the phone, "Hi, Teresa," he said. He called me Teresa, the only name he and my mother ever used.

"Is Dorothy all right?" I said.

"She's waiting to say hello."

I'd never been happier to hear my sister-in-law's voice. "I'm so glad you called," I said and then I told her about my going out to dinner with Herb. "It's the first time I've been out since I lost Frank."

"You go and have a wonderful time, dear," Dorothy said. "Frank would want you to go out. Remember, I told you Herb would be a good friend."

My heart was much lighter when I heard Herb's knock on the door. We went to a lovely restaurant in Palo Alto where we enjoyed a relaxing drink in the bar before dinner. We talked about our families and got to know a little more about each other.

Herb was Jewish, born in New York. He lived there until he went into the Army. After four years of duty in the Pacific, he enrolled at the University of Wisconsin. He was able to put himself through college on the GI Bill, graduating in 1950 as a chemical engineer. Herb now worked at Lockheed in Sunnyvale as a staff scientist. He married in 1956 and divorced a few years later. He had no children. His mother lived in Florida. The rest of his family still lived in New York.

I talked a lot about Frank and the boys while we enjoyed dinner. Herb was a good listener. He seemed like a very sincere man. I felt comfortable with him.

Herb was interested to hear about the trimaran. As he drove me home, he asked if I would like to join him the next morning when he went to check on his sailboat.

"My boat is docked at Pacific Marina, one of the harbors in Alameda, across the Bay from San Francisco."

He told me he was a member of the Oakland Yacht Club that used to be in Oakland, but moved to Alameda when the club built a new clubhouse.

"We decided not to change the name."

The next morning, Herb arrived at the house early wearing casual clothes and a big smile. "We may not have a lot of wind for sailing, but at least the sun's shining. I thought we'd have breakfast on the way." He advised me to bring a jacket and to wear rubber-soled shoes.

Herb and I were like a couple of kids as we chatted over a breakfast at a coffee shop along the way. When we arrived at the Pacific Marina in Alameda, the number of boats docked in the harbor amazed me.

"This is just one marina. There're many more in this area," Herb said. "Now be careful going down the ramp. The tide's out and it's pretty steep."

"Don't worry, I used to be a dancer so I'm pretty sure-footed," I said. At that moment, I lost my footing. Herb grabbed my arm to keep me from slipping. We have laughed about that many times.

When we came to his 22′ Santana sailboat, Herb said, "There she is, Golconda II. Hop aboard."

I sat in the cockpit as Herb took the hatch covers off the sails. His small sailboat was immaculate. Below deck were a tiny galley and a comfortable-looking berth. I had to laugh when Herb said, "You look right at home on this boat."

"That's funny," I said. "I've never been on a sailboat before that was in the water."

"You mean you and Frank were building that big trimaran and you've never sailed?"

We had a wonderful day on his boat. Herb had been sailing all his life. Golconda II was his fourth boat. She was equipped with every possible safety feature and was well-maintained. We motored out of the slip into the estuary. I knew I was in expert hands as I watched Herb handle the boat.

I fell in love with the little sailboat. I could tell Herb was an experienced sailor. When we were in the Bay, Herb turned the motor off and hoisted the sails. The tranquility was breathtaking. I decided then I would learn to sail.

Herb and I were tired but happy as we drove home. Herb said goodnight and promised to call. As I climbed into bed, I felt more at peace than I had for months.

At the end of the week, Herb called me at the office. "Are you ready for a sailing lesson?"

I tried not to sound too anxious, but I couldn't keep the excitement out of my voice as I accepted his invitation. I wasn't really sure if it was the boat or Herb that I wanted to see most. I couldn't wait for Sunday morning.

I soon discovered that sailing wasn't as easy as I'd imagined. As we headed out of the estuary into the Bay, I found that fast responses to orders were necessary because tides and winds could be unpredictable.

In spite of Herb barking orders and expecting me to be sure of my actions, I knew that if I wanted to sail, and I did, Herb would be a great teacher. Already the feel of the wind in my face and the quietness of the boat moving through the water gave me the exhilaration I needed to begin living again.

A few weeks later, I decided to enroll in a boating course at De Anza College. I would learn about tides, buoys, navigation, anchoring, rules of the road and sailing vocabulary. I've never been a student, except in dancing. I found the course extremely interesting. I passed the required exam at the completion of the course. Herb was impressed and delighted when I told him I'd taken the course.

Herb had a lot of friends at the Oakland Yacht Club. They made me feel very welcome. As the weeks went by, a new world opened up for me. Herb and I spent every Saturday at the harbor. Herb came for dinner on Wednesday nights. He always went to the gym after work, so dinner was late.

I sensed that Herb was afraid of becoming too involved. He didn't say much about his past, but I knew he didn't want another marriage. I told him that I understood and was happy to enjoy our friendship. I didn't want another marriage, either. I was sure I could never be as happy as I was with Frank. Herb's companionship was all I thought I needed to fill the void in my life.

But as the months flew by, I realized I was falling in love with Herb. I enjoyed having someone to share things with and to plan dinners for on Wednesdays. Each time I answered the phone at the office on Fridays, I hoped I'd hear Herb's voice inviting me for dinner at his apartment, and most Fridays I wasn't disappointed.

Herb was extremely independent and although he didn't discuss his past, it was obvious he'd been hurt and he'd built a wall around himself that he wouldn't let anyone penetrate. He was a warm, friendly person with expressive brown eyes and a charming smile, generous and intelligent. I knew he was a loving person, but I also knew I'd have to be patient and wait until he was ready to let his defenses down.

I loved sailing on Golconda II. With Herb's expert teaching, I was becoming a good sailor.

In May 1973, I received a call from the young couple who had bought the trimaran. They told me they were going to launch her and wanted me to come to the christening. I called Herb to ask if he'd take me to Alviso. I knew I'd need some moral support as the big boat was lowered into the water. Herb agreed. The following Saturday, we drove to Alviso. The tide would not be high until after ten that evening.

When Herb and I arrived at the marina in Alviso, George and Jean were already there, celebrating the occasion by drinking Cold Duck. They were so proud when they took me on board to see the results of their efforts. They hadn't finished the interior as perfectly as I knew Frank would have, but it was comfortable and well-planned for living on board. I was grateful the young couple had completed Frank's and my dream.

I was glad to enjoy a couple of glasses of Cold Duck to relax me. I listened to the excited young people as they told of their plans for the trimaran and their future. When they named her "Cold Duck," I knew the boat was really theirs. They'd chosen a name quite different from what Frank and I had planned.

Finally, the tide was right. We watched Jean break a bottle of champagne across the bow. We held our breaths as Cold Duck slipped gracefully into the water. Tears clouded my vision. I felt Herb's arm around me and I buried my head on his shoulder. I thanked God for the understanding of this kind man.

George and Jean promised to keep in touch with me. I gave each of them a hug and wished them the very best luck as I turned to look at our trimaran for the last time.

In June 1973, Charlie called to tell me that Dorothy was paralyzed and not doing well on her medication. "I'm coming to Winnipeg," I told him. "I'll let you know when to meet me."

Dr. Abramson closed the office for a week. The next Monday, Herb drove me to the airport and promised to pick me up the following Friday night. As the plane flew over the Bay, I looked down at all the little white dots floating on the water. I felt a tug at my heart as I thought about Golconda II. I'd be sailing on her the following weekend.

When Charlie met the plane, I could see the strain he was under by the lines on his face. He took me in his arms. "Hi, Teresa. It's so wonderful to see you."

I hoped I'd be able to give him the support he had shown me in 1944 when we were in England together.

As we drove to the house, I was amazed to see how much Winnipeg had changed; many new buildings and dozens of housing developments.

"You'll be staying with May," Charlie told me. Dorothy's unable to leave her bed and I don't share the room with her because it would be too uncomfortable for her. Would you like to go directly to May's?"

"No, Charlie. I want to see Dorothy first."

"Hi, dear," I heard Dorothy call from her bedroom. I hurried in to my sister-in-law. Dorothy looked radiant as she held her arms out to me. She felt thin when I hugged her. Dorothy said, "Now, tell me about your sailing and the boys. How is Grant? And how is Herb?"

I talked for a while, but I didn't want to tire Dorothy. I told her, "I'll answer some questions now and save some for tomorrow. I've so much to tell you. Charlie will take me to May's now, but I'll come over tomorrow. You get a good night's sleep and be ready for a long talk in the morning."

May seemed happy to have me stay with her. She was still the same sweet woman, but she'd aged considerably since I'd last seen her. We sat up late that night and May cried as she told me how lost she was without Pud.

"I understand what you're going through. Loosing Frank was so hard," I said.

"You're lucky, Terrie, to have found someone to help you enjoy life again," May said.

"May, I never believed I could be this happy again. My time with Herb is always wonderful, yet it doesn't take anything away from my memories of my life with Frank. It's like starting all over again. However, even though I'm sure I love Herb, I'm not so sure he feels the same way about me. I know he's very fond of me, but he has a lot of things to resolve. I'm not sure he'll ever make a commitment, but I don't really mind as long as we continue our relationship."

I loved the time I spent in Winnipeg, seeing old friends and visiting relatives. Maude still had her flower shop. I sensed some disapproval when I mentioned my relationship with Herb.

Tony, Dorothy's son, had a lovely wife, Heather, and I finally got to meet Dorothy's granddaughter, Christine. Dorothy and Charlie really enjoyed their granddaughter. My heart ached as I knew when I left I'd say goodbye to all of them for the last time. Charlie offered to take me to see the stone they'd put on the grave where Frank's ashes had been buried.

I explained to Charlie that seeing the stone would not mean anything to me. I wanted to remember Frank as he was when we were together. Seeing that stone would be too depressing.

As I said goodbye and we embraced, Dorothy whispered in my ear, "If Charlie needs help, I know you'll be there. You take care and enjoy life, dear. Say hello to Herb and thank him for me. I know he'll look after you and so I won't worry about you."

It was hard, but I didn't look back when Charlie and I left the room. As we drove to the airport, I said, "Dorothy's the most unselfish person I've ever known. I feel privileged to be related to her. Charlie, you know I'll always be here if you need me."

As the plane took off, I knew another era in my life was over. I wouldn't be coming back to Winnipeg. Dorothy died a few weeks later. I was so grateful to have seen her before she passed away.

Left: We were sailing toward
the Golden Gate Bridge,
heading out to sea.

Above: Herb's a happy sailor.
At the harbor after a day of
sailing.

At the Delta. On a cruise with the Oakland Yacht Club members.

Left: Herb directing me at the helm, while he was adjusting the rigging.

Below right: Sailing on San Francisco Bay.

Below left: Herb enjoying a day at sea.

*Right: We always had time for a
hug, in spite of heavy winds.*

*Below: Pacific Marina is in
Alameda on the Oakland Estuary.
After docking Golconda III, we
enjoyed relaxing.*

Herb's and my wedding, February 1975. A wonderful beginning of a new chapter in our lives.

Chapter 11

Christmas 1973 was lonely. Herb went on a sailing trip in the Caribbean with three of his relatives.

Brock, Karen and Kent came home for the holiday. Grant was 14 months old, walking and trying to talk—a really cute little boy.

Kent and Sharon were still seeing a lot of each other, but Kent was not ready to settle down. Sharon wrote a note to me saying she was sorry Kent had decided to go to Alaska so far away, but she would wait for him. They were young and I knew when the time was right, things would work out for them.

I didn't want Kent to leave, but I remembered Frank saying travel was a good education. I knew my youngest son was still restless and had to get it out of his system.

Karen and Brock were trying to make things work, but their marriage was in trouble. I had hoped having Grant would make things better between them, but they even disagreed on how to raise Grant. I didn't want Grant to grow up in an unhappy house. I wished I hadn't urged Brock to not give up on his marriage when he was home before Frank died.

When Herb returned home from his sailing trip, he seemed really glad to see me. He took me in his arms, and said, "You look great, kid. I really missed you. We had a great time, but we sure could have used an experienced sailor like you."

I hadn't realized how much I'd missed Herb until then. However, I could sense something different in Herb's attitude. He seemed to be more evasive and quiet. I caught him pondering more than usual. We still spent weekends together at the harbor, and most Wednesdays we enjoyed dinner and the evening at my house. Yet, something was different about Herb that mystified me.

Early that spring, Herb and I were sailing on San Francisco Bay. As we enjoyed the perfect weather, I looked across the tranquil waters. Suddenly, I cried out. "Herb, there's Cold Duck."

"No, Terrie, you're wrong," Herb said.

"Herb," I said, "that boat was in my backyard for nine years and I'd know her anywhere. Please try to sail closer to that trimaran."

As Herb maneuvered his boat, I didn't lose sight of the impressive sailboat with her sails full, racing across San Francisco Bay. When we were close enough, we could read the words Cold Duck on her transom.

The tears of joy rolled down my face as I watched Frank's dream come true. Our trimaran was actually sailing on San Francisco Bay. I prayed Frank could see her as she cut proudly through the water.

Herb put his arms around me and said, "Terrie, this is a day you'll never forget. What an amazing coincidence."

A few months later, when I received a ship's log from the Barnes, I was so excited to read that they had sailed to Mexico on Cold Duck with no problems. They told me the only weak thing on the boat was the crew. They were planning more off-shore sailing before trying to sail to Hawaii. I didn't hear from them again, but a few years later I learned that Cold Duck was in San Diego being refurbished. I was satisfied. Frank's work had been proven seaworthy and his work was not in vain.

Although I didn't tell my sons, I knew Herb was in love with me. As Christmas 1974 drew near, Herb told me he planned to meet his family in Florida in December. His mother lived in Miami Beach and his sister, Adelaide, and his brother-in-law, Charlie, were also going to visit, along with their son Scott and a recently-widowed friend, Judy Schaffer.

"Would you consider going with me?" Herb asked. "You could share a room with Judy, and Scott and I could stay together. I would like you to meet my family."

"Well, I've never been away from my family during the holidays," I replied. "But, Kent will be in Alaska and I'm sure Karen, Brock and Grant will be spending the day with Karen's folks, so let me think about it for a day or so."

A few days later, I got a surprise when I heard from Kent. "Hi, Mom. Guess what? I'm back in Redding." He never ceased to amaze me with his travels. I knew he was leaving Alaska, but I thought he would be coming to Sunnyvale. "I do want to see you, Mom," but he told me Sharon's family had invited him for Christmas and he planned to stay in Redding and go to college there. He also would look for part-time work.

So, things worked out for me. With both boys away for the holiday, I decided I could go to Florida. I was happy that Herb wanted me to meet his family, but I wondered if they would approve of me as I was not Jewish.

I did not have to worry. When I met Herb's mother, she greeted me warmly and we had a wonderful visit. She told me all about Herb when he was a child and young man growing up. The tiny woman was so warmhearted and had a wonderful sense of humor. I could see where Herb had inherited his sincerity.

Adelaide and Charlie were a fun couple. They made me feel right at home when we got back to the hotel in Miami. They introduced me to Judy. She was quite distant, but I could relate to that since she had just lost her husband.

Herb's nephew, Scott, arrived and after giving Uncle Herb a warm hug, he gave me one, too. Scott was very fond of his uncle. A fine young man, handsome with dark wavy hair. Scott was studying to become a dental surgeon. Herb had taken Scott sailing on the Bay when he visited Herb in California.

I called the boys on Christmas Day and everyone seemed to be happy and enjoying the holiday. That's when I began to realize that things can't always stay the same.

Herb took me to the Everglades and some other interesting places in Florida before we headed home to California. We visited many of the crowded harbors. I discovered how great Florida was for sailing. The days were wonderful, but the nights, sharing a room with Judy, were not so happy. Judy talked about how lonely she was and how fortunate I was to have Herb. I reminded her that Herb and I were just friends. "I don't think Herb will marry again, but we enjoy the same things and I'm content with our arrangement."

During our visit with Herb's family, I told them stories about my family as they did about theirs. We laughed a lot. Before we left, I made them promise to come to California before too long.

I was very fortunate to have Herb's companionship. I also knew our relationship could end since Herb seemed so afraid to let me know his feelings. Despite those feelings on both of our parts, we had a happy vacation and I began to realize another thing during that Christmas holiday—life changes.

When we returned to San Francisco, life went on as before. We went to the harbor on the weekends. I was becoming an adept sailor with Herb's teaching. I really loved his little sailboat and was learning more about handling the lines, hoisting the sails and also boating terminology. Herb was a strict tutor. He was also a careful sailor. He had learned to sail as a boy when he joined the Sea Scouts.

I felt no concern, even in the rough weather, with Herb at the helm. My strong feelings for Herb continued to grow.

When we didn't sail, we visited boatyards looking at boats. Early in January 1975, we were walking around the harbor when I spotted a beautiful 30' boat with a "For sale" sign on her bow.

"That's an Islander," Herb said. "They're great boats. I'm surprised to see one for sale. Let's see if we can find the harbor master or the broker and take a look at her."

We were fortunate to find the broker with a key and so we boarded the boat. We were impressed when we went below and saw the beautiful teak cabin. The boat was roomy. The V-berth had cabinets below the sleeping area and shelves on either side. The layout below really impressed me. The small, adequate toilet space had a stainless steel wash basin with a mirror and cabinet hanging over it. The main cabin had shelving above the bunks with room for a TV, plus a clock and fathometer. The bunks on either side of the cabin had been upholstered in blue leather and the narrow windows had blue-and-white pleated curtains. I loved those colors.

We found that the left side bunk had an opening at the end where a tall person could put his feet when sleeping. The kitchen had a stainless steel sink with drawers and shelves for food storage. Herb was really impressed with the layout. He told the broker the sailboat appeared to be strongly constructed. "This is a great boat," he said. "I'm excited about it. I have to get hold of the owner."

After inspecting below deck, Herb checked out the bilge and the top deck. The hull was painted white, the deck a pale blue. She was perfect.

"This was the first boat the owner ever bought," the broker told us. "She's just eleven months old and has never been sailed. The owner's wife is afraid of the water and he decided he doesn't enjoy being out in the elements."

"It has a lot of very good features," Herb said. "I'd like the name of the owner so we can arrange to go for a sail with him."

I was excited, too. I also felt a little worried. "What will you do with the Golconda II?"

"Well, if I decide to buy this boat, I'd have to sell her. It's not a good idea to have two boats."

That made me sad. I'd learned to sail on that little boat. I always felt so comfortable on her. I knew that hoisting the sails and putting a bigger vessel into a slip would be more of a challenge for me.

Herb did get hold of the young man who owned the Islander and arranged to meet him the following Saturday to go for a sail. After sailing with the boat owner, Herb told me he could understand the fellow wanting to sell the Islander. The man apparently knew nothing about sailing, especially on San Francisco Bay. He told Herb he bought the boat as a tax write-off and had no idea what he was getting into. He and his wife would be glad to sell her. Herb called me when he got home to say that he'd bought the boat. He told me the boat handled beautifully and he could hardly wait to take me aboard.

When Herb put an ad in the paper to sell his Santana, he received calls from a number of interested people who wanted to see the sailboat. He made appointments with two couples for the following Sunday.

The first couple to look at the little Santana offered Herb cash, which he was ready to accept, but I had talked to another couple who I knew were anxious to have the Santana. Unfortunately, this couple would have a hard time raising the cash. I asked Herb to consider letting them have a few days to try.

"Well, kid," he said. Herb always called me kid. I guess that was a New York expression. "The first people have the cash. I may be making a mistake, but I'll go along with you."

"I know they'll find the money, Herb, and they'll take good care of Golconda. She's so important to me that I want her to be loved by the person who buys her. Please give them a chance. They seem so right to me."

The Golconda II was like a true friend. Whoever bought her would have to treat her well and enjoy her like I had.

My instincts were right. Herb called me at the office three days later to tell me the young couple had raised the money and they would meet him at the harbor with a check on the following Saturday.

Herb and I were really impressed with the way the Islander sailed and on January 13, 1974, Herb took possession of his new boat. He asked me what he should name her. The boat was named Sunshine. That didn't suit Herb or the boat.

"Well, I suggest that since Golconda is the name of a mine in India, and it means 'a wealth of pleasure,' I think she should be named Golconda III."

So, the 30' Islander was rechristened Golconda III and soon I found that hoisting the sails and handling the lines was much harder on a larger boat. Herb even taught me how to put the boat in and out of its slip; he had a lot of confidence in me.

Later that month, I was polishing the brass, oiling the teak and cleaning the life lines when I felt Herb's arms around me. I was really shocked when I heard him say, "You know, kid, I've loved you for a long time. I think it's time we got married."

I could hardly believe my ears. I had decided Herb and I were enjoying our time together and I would be satisfied to go on the way we were. I knew he never wanted to be married, so I'd resigned myself to the fact that he'd never propose to me.

"I'd love to marry you," I said, then turned to kiss him. We went below deck and hugged each other. We were laughing and crying at the same time. I'll never forget those moments.

"Let's plan on February 15th, that is, if you're not busy that day."

"February 15th sounds wonderful, but why that day?"

"It's the day after Valentine's Day and I'll always be able to remember our anniversary. Also, that's a Saturday, so it won't be a problem for you to get away from the office. Besides, kid, I don't want to wait any longer."

When I returned to the house after the weekend, I looked around the living room and went into the bedroom and finally into the back garden. In my heart I knew I was doing the right thing. I told myself that Frank would be happy, too. He wouldn't have wanted me to spend my life alone. He knew I would always keep him in my heart. However, a whole new world had opened up to me since meeting Herb. Being involved in sailing, it would be a different kind of marriage. We wouldn't be struggling to make ends meet. We wouldn't be raising children. We'd appreciate what we each accomplished, and of course, we wouldn't be building a boat. I promised myself that I would try to make this marriage a good one. I knew I could make Herb happy.

Brock and Karen were delighted when I called them with the news. They both liked Herb. Little Grant adored him. When I called Kent, he told me, "Herb's a great guy, Mom. I'm so happy to know you'll be taken care of. He'll always be a friend, but don't expect me to have him take Dad's place."

"Herb won't try to take your father's place, Kent, but I hope you'll consider him to be more than a friend. He'll be your stepfather."

When Herb and I told our friends the news, they all agreed it was about time. Herb's family was delighted, too. When we applied for our marriage license, we got quite a surprise. The document they gave us had sailboats printed on it.

"This must be a good luck omen," Herb said. "Our marriage was meant to be."

We decided on a quiet wedding in Pacific Grove, a small town on the ocean near Monterey. Herb called the Chamber of Commerce and was given the name of a Justice of the Peace there. Herb contacted Mr. Vit, who agreed to marry us the following Saturday, February 15, 1975.

We asked our mutual friends, Marie and Frank Spillane, to come with us to Pacific Grove to be our witnesses. They readily agreed.

My good friends, Gloria and Ed Miller, offered to have a reception the day after our wedding. I called all my close friends and Herb gave me a list of friends he'd like invited. Brock, Karen and Grant would come from Sacramento where they now lived, and Kent and Sharon would come from Redding.

The night before our wedding, I decided what I must do. I made a cup of tea and built a fire. While I sat in the house I'd lived in for 23 years, I took out the little sewing box that Edith had given me many years before that I called my treasure box. Inside I found the little teddy bear I'd given Frank. Teddy looked a bit ragged. And in the box were letters Frank had written to me when I was in England trying to get to Canada in 1944. I also found the little heart- shaped box that held my engagement ring.

As I read Frank's letters, the 30 years seemed to fade away and the memories of those times seemed like yesterday. After I read each one, I threw it into the flames. I'd always have those memories, I knew. However, that needed to be put in the past where it belonged if I was to start a new life with Herb.

I took off my wedding band and put it in the little box with my engagement ring. Along with those precious memories, I placed my prayer book Mom and Dad had given me, the certificate from the judge that gave me permission to marry Frank, plus a few other mementos, in my treasure box and closed the lid.

I went to bed, knowing a new chapter in my life was just beginning. How fortunate I was to have another loving partner to share my life with.

When I awoke on my wedding day, I was happy to see a warm, sunny morning. I showered, dressed in my new light weight knit suit I'd picked because Herb's favorite color was pale mauve, and greeted Herb who'd arrived in the driveway. He had a happy smile on his face as he greeted me with a kiss. "Happy wedding day, kid," he said.

We were like a couple of youngsters as we drove to pick up Marie and Frank Spillane. I had known them before because Frank had worked with my Frank at Hewlett-Packard. Since Herb and I had spent a lot of time with Marie and Frank, I was pleased to have them as our witnesses. We picked them up at their home in Sunnyvale and the four of us enjoyed the lovely drive to Pacific Grove, a little town near Carmel.

Marie gave me a beautiful bouquet of white roses and carnations. The scent of the flowers filled the car.

We arrived in Monterey in time for lunch before we drove on to Pacific Grove. Mr. Vit lived in a charming little house. He greeted us with a friendly smile.

After we introduced ourselves, Mr. Vit took Marie and me to a room where I could change into the floor length dress I'd chosen for the ceremony. The lines of the dress were very plain. The aqua colored crepe fell softly as I walked into the living room to meet Herb.

"You look beautiful, kid," Herb told me as he took my hand.

We stood in front of Mr. Vit with Frank and Marie on either side.
As music played softly, the ceremony began.

Mr. Vit spoke the words with sincerity and when he
pronounced us husband and wife, I turned to Herb. We kissed
and at that moment, I knew how much I loved him. I promised
myself I would always try to make him happy.

As we talked with Mr. Vit, I discovered this interesting man
had been involved with the Danish Underground in World War II.
He knew many of the airmen who I remembered reading about in
the war years.

Before going to dinner on the wharf, we went to see the
famous Monarch Butterflies that migrate to Pacific Grove every
February to hatch their eggs in the eucalyptus and pine trees. The
butterflies awed me with their brilliant colors as thousands of
them covered the branches, a truly incredible sight.

We chose Pacific Grove for our wedding because it's near the
ocean and we had many memories of being in that area together.

After dropping Marie and Frank at their home in Sunnyvale,
we said our goodbyes and thanked them for being our witnesses.
They both agreed the day had been perfect.

Herb had reserved a suite at the Cabana Hotel in Palo Alto.
The grounds were lovely. Fountains sat on either side of the wide
driveway leading to the hotel entrance.

I had a hard time believing this was all happening to me.
By now, it had been almost three years since Frank had died. At
that time, I thought life was never going to be the same. Now,
here I was married and starting life over with Herb. I felt like the
luckiest woman in the world.

Herb had champagne brought to our suite and as we toasted
each other, he said, "Here's to a long, happy life together, kid. I

want you to know that I'll always love you. I hope your sons know that, too."

I had tears in my eyes when I replied. "Herb, I promise I will always do my very best to make you happy."

The next morning, we went back to my house to wait for the family. Brock and Karen arrived with Grant. My grandson was an active two-year-old with an infectious smile.

Before long, Kent and Sharon drove up. They looked happy together. I could see how much they enjoyed each other. Sharon came from a delightful family in Redding. Kent had introduced us when we visited him there.

I could sense that things had not improved between Brock and Karen. They were cold to each other. Even having Grant had not helped improve their relationship. I was concerned, but I decided they'd work things out. This was going to be a wonderful day to start my life with Herb. Both boys liked Herb, which was a blessing to me.

After a great family get-together, we all drove to Gloria and Ed Miller's home in Sunnyvale. Gloria and Ed had arranged a wedding reception for Herb and me. When we arrived we were greeted by many of my old and dear friends, and some of Herb's friends who I had met recently.

What a truly joyous occasion. Gloria and Shirley had shared in making the food and the champagne flowed freely.

My mind went back to Frank and our wedding reception in Winnipeg when I didn't know anyone and hardly knew Frank. We'd not been together for 15 months. This time, I had family with me.

Brock proposed a toast to our happiness and as Herb and I cut our wedding cake, I knew a new and exciting chapter in my life was just beginning.

Kent brought Sharon home for Christmas in 1977 and they announced their engagement. We were delighted as we loved Sharon. She had waited patiently for five years until Kent was ready to marry her.

"We'll be married in Redding on May 27th. We want the ceremony to be outside in a park that's in a lovely area with a stream running through huge oak trees," Sharon said. "My parents will give us a reception at the Moose Lodge in Redding. They're so happy for us. They love Kent."

The next few months were busy as the family prepared for the wedding.

"Kent, I'd like to give you and Sharon a rehearsal dinner," Herb said. "Please tell me a nice place in Redding we can arrange to have the entire wedding party for a formal dinner."

"Well, we do have a favorite spot. It's called Bridge Bay and it overlooks Lake Shasta."

Herb made the arrangements. That evening, before dinner was served, Kent stood with glass in hand and said, "I'd like to propose a toast to Herb Dorfman, a man who has proved that everyone has a second chance."

My family was complete once again.

Postscript

It is amazing how circumstances change one's life. I enjoyed writing my memoir, reliving the experiences, the choices and decisions I made along the way. And remembering the people who influenced me.

Jim Edgar hired me to work at the Y, knowing I lied about my age. That job allowed me to meet Frank.

When the judge gave me permission to get married, I realized that anything can be possible. And as proof, the Canadian Consulate gave me permission to leave England during the war when civilians weren't allowed to leave.

Dr. Abramson gave me the opportunity to work for him even though I had no experience in a medical office. If Herb had not been his patient, I would not have met him or known about his interest in sailing.

If Herb had not been a sailor, I would never have had the thrill of seeing Frank's trimaran sailing on San Francisco Bay.

The person who influenced my life more than any other was my dear nursemaid, Edith. She would have been proud to know my dancing school was successful and that I had found such joy through the years.

Maude, the last of Frank's brothers and sisters who took me into their lives and offered me their love, died at 83.

In 2002, my sister Kathleen called to say my brother Bill had died quite suddenly. Marjorie died a year later. Richard was killed in a car accident in 1981, just 33 years old, leaving Katie with two small boys. Kathleen's husband, Phil, died in 1988. She and I are the only ones left of our family. We've become very close over the years. On her first visit with us, I remarked, "How come we're so much closer now than we ever were before?"

"We grew up," she replied.

As 2011 comes to a close, I have three grandchildren —Grant, Kylie and Garret, and 4 great grandsons—Marcus, Chase, Carter and a new baby boy, Casen.

Frank's memory is always with us. The grandchildren love Grandpa Herb, but they know Grandpa Frank was their other grandpa by the pictures we show them and the stories we tell.

My 36 years with Herb have been full of adventure, wonderful sailing experiences, travel and joy in watching our family grow. We sold Golconda III in 2007, an extremely hard decision for the two of us.

The loss of my parents and my disappointment that they did not live to see their grandchildren are always with me.

I still struggle as I continue to ask myself if there had been any other way to be with Frank and to obey my parent's demands at the same time.

My answer has never changed. I did what I had to do. Even though the hurt does not go away, I have no regrets. I navigated my life the best I could, following my true bearing.

www.ingramcontent.com/pod-product-compliance
Lightning Source LLC
La Vergne TN
LVHW011222080426
835509LV00005B/268